THE
LAST WORD

Selected Columns from the
Editor of The Baptist Courier

THE LAST WORD

Selected Columns from the
Editor of The Baptist Courier

JAMES RUDY GRAY

The Last Word: Selected Columns from the Editor of The Baptist Courier

Copyright © 2022 James Rudy Gray

All Rights Reserved

Scripture taken from the New American Standard Bible,
Copyright © 1960, 1962, 1963, 1972, 1973, 1975, 1977, 1995 by
The Lockman Foundation. Used by permission. wwwLockman.org.

ISBN 978-1-955295-22-2

Courier Publishing
100 Manly Street
Greenville, South Carolina 29601
CourierPublishing.com

Published in the United States of America

Dedication

This book of columns is dedicated to the tremendous staff of The Baptist Courier. Their great work ethic and godly attitude cannot be duplicated, but it can be admired!

Thank you for a decade of blessings.

Foreword

Rudy Gray has served South Carolina Baptists well for over ten years as editor of The Courier. His impact on South Carolina Baptist life goes well beyond that decade and will continue for years to come. His years of experience as a pastor, leader and statesman — along with his gift and training as a journalist — is why is he is so effective in telling the stories of God at work, not only here at home, but around the nation and world as well.

Other than the administrative gifts necessary to lead a top-notch ministry like The Courier, the power of the pen, through editorials, serves to encourage, inspire, inform and, at times, challenge the reader. This collection of "the best of Rudy Gray" over the past ten years will continue to bring his writing to life for generations to come.

You will laugh, you will cry, and at times you may sigh, but mainly you will be blessed as you read these articles. Our South Carolina Baptist family holds the distinction of being the first state convention within our larger Southern Baptist Convention family of churches, but The Courier holds the unique honor of being the first Baptist publication. If the Lord should tarry His coming another 200 years, we pray The Courier will still be telling the Good News stories of God at work in South Carolina and beyond. If so, future generations of South Carolina Baptists will be standing on the shoulders of gifted and godly leaders like Rudy Gray!

Gary Hollingsworth, Executive Director-Treasurer
South Carolina Baptist Convention

Table of Contents

The Influence of Tim Tebow 3
Receiving and Giving Care 5
Healthy Marriages and Compatibility 7
The Great Commission Is Not the Main Thing 9
Is Biblical Preaching Relevant Today? 12
Remember to Care 14
Easter Is Personal 17
The Graying of America and What It Means 19
Encouraging One Another 22
Freedom-Fed Patriotism 25
Domestic Abuse Is Sin 27
Ministering to Addicts 30
Jesus Is Salvation — Anything Else Is Counterfeit 33
The Privilege of Having a Good Mother 35
True Champions for Christ 38
The Confederate Flag Is Out, But Is Racial Reconciliation In? 41
Adoption ... It's Personal 43
The Blessing of Friendship 45
Blessed Resurrection Day! 48
The Importance of Biblical Truth 50
Even in Retirement, Be Sure to Live Until You Die 53
The Thanksgiving Lady 55
The Season We Call Christmas 57
Living in 'Post-Truth' Times 60
Counting Your Blessings 63
What a Providential Time for Gospel Conversations 65
Detours on the Roman Road 68

What a Great Name for a Pastor	71
A Christmas Eve Near the Moon	73
Alzheimer's Didn't Win	76
It's More than St. Patrick's Day	79
Gratitude for God's Mercy	81
The Power of Theology Is Applying It	83
Remembering September 11	85
Don't Overlook Pastor Appreciation	88
God's Adventurous Missionary	90
It's Time to Rejoice!	92
One Solitary Life	94
Angels and Death	97
We Need Godly Fathers	99
The Greatest Generation	102
The Thinking Christian	105
To Boomer	108
The Buckley Legacy	111
Resolutions or Renewals?	113
The Virtue of Waiting	116
Tribute to Bill Adams	119
The Month of August	121
Gen Z Christians Show Potential	123
Keep On Keeping On	126

THE
LAST WORD

Selected Columns from the
Editor of The Baptist Courier

February 2013

The Influence of Tim Tebow

Influence is that personal power, moral persuasion or spiritual force that has an effect on another person.

Tim Tebow has influence. In 2012, he made Time magazine's list of the 100 most influential people in the world. While playing football, he has worn eye-black strips printed with Scripture references and often takes a knee in a gesture of prayer during a game. He has made strong and clear public expressions of his faith in Jesus Christ.

Does it make any difference? According to a Barna Group survey released in February, it may not make as much difference as we think.

The Barna report revealed that "most Americans believe when an athlete talks about his or her faith publicly, it does not make much of a difference for those who hear those comments."

However, about 32 percent said those public displays of faith by athletes do influence the hearers to be more spiritually minded. The 32 percent was composed of women, Southern residents, evangelicals and church attenders.

In other words, those of us who already believe like to see these public expressions of faith. The actual influence on unbelievers may not be nearly as great as we hope.

Tebow's mom, Pam, has stressed the importance of using our influence to share the gospel. Her son does that. However, his greatest influence publicly may be his stance on moral issues. During her pregnancy with Tim, Pam risked her life to give birth to her son. In her mind, abortion was not an option. A 2010 Super Bowl ad featured Tebow and his mother sharing a pro-life message. According to Barna, the ad resulted in 5.5 million people "having cause to rethink their stand on abortion."

Tebow is more recognized for his Christian faith than any other professional athlete: 83 percent of Americans are aware of him, and 73 percent feel favorably about his public discussion of faith. What the survey reveals is that most Americans, especially Christians, have a high regard for an authentic role model who connects faith and life.

Does Tebow have influence? Absolutely. In fact, many people believe he has more influence on society than pastors. The Barna survey reported that "overall, about two-thirds (64 percent) of Americans say they think pro athletes have more influence in American society today than do professional faith leaders (19 percent)."

Do Tebow's public expressions of faith connect lost people to the gospel? We don't really know. The survey only records what people thought. It seems it would be impossible to measure that in any kind of objective way.

Tebow's decision last week to cancel a speaking engagement at First Baptist Church in Dallas has disheartened those who believe he did so under the pressure of political correctness. Other evangelical leaders, however, believe Tebow has earned the benefit of the doubt.

In pulling out of his appearance, Tebow took to Twitter to explain himself: "While I was looking forward to sharing a message of hope and Christ's unconditional love — due to new information that has been brought to my attention, I have decided to cancel my upcoming appearance. I will continue to use the platform God has blessed me with to bring Faith, Hope and Love to all those needing a brighter day."

While Tebow's decision is disappointing, it doesn't change the fact that he has influence, and influence can be used for good or bad. May he continue to use his platform to share the good news of Christ with all who are watching and listening.

January 2014

Receiving and Giving Care

My dad passed away a few years ago. Today, my mom, who has Alzheimer's, lives in an assisted living home near us. Neither of my parents ever wanted to be a burden to anyone, but we wanted to provide the help they needed and to do our best to care for them personally at a time when they were unable to care for themselves.

One of my daughters recently shared with me that she would be "taking care of me someday." My response was, "No. I will not be a burden to you." Then I made some remark about getting on an ice float and floating away. While I was joking, there is usually some element of truth in our humor.

What makes us say we don't want to be a burden to our children? Maybe it's pride, suggests Russell Moore. "I want to live with the image in my loved ones' memories of me as in my prime," he wrote on his website, "Moore to the Point," in May 2013. "I don't want the humiliation of having to be cared for in my weakness, or the fearfulness of having to trust someone else to attend to my needs. I want to be a man, but I don't want to be a helpless baby in need of parents or a helpless elder in need of my children."

From conception to natural death, we need the help of others. It seems we start out being dependent on people, and we end our journey again dependent on people. Today, my mother does not remember much. I have spoken with her many times about her relationship with Christ, and every time, she talks about going to heaven because of Him. A few times I have asked her to sing a hymn with me. Recently, my wife surreptitiously videoed (with her phone) my mom and me singing "Amazing Grace" together. It was very light on talent, but it is a memory I will cherish. The next day, my mom didn't remember it, but I did.

As Moore points out, "In the Body of Christ, there are not people who have burdens and people who don't. We are to 'bear one another's burdens' (Galatians 6:2). We are all a burden to be borne, just in different ways." Choosing not to be a burden to anyone is noble thinking, perhaps, but knowing we are, or will be, a burden to some degree is a reality.

We celebrate the sanctity of human life this month because we are made in the image of God, but we live out the principle of the sacredness of life when we realize the need to care for others and to be cared for by others.

Life is precious and sacred. The older I get, the more loved ones I have in heaven. One day, I will see a brother and sister who died as infants. I will see the two babies we miscarried and our two grandchildren who were miscarried. Their lives began at conception. I will see loved ones who lived long lives before they died. The magnificence of seeing Jesus will put everything into a glorious perspective.

Charles Weigle was a Baptist evangelist and songwriter who was born in 1871 and died in 1966. He wrote more than 1,000 hymns and Christian songs. During his ministry, his wife left him and later died. He spent several years in such despondency that he contemplated suicide. He questioned if anyone really cared for him. Through time, God restored his faith and his ministry. One day, in less than 20 minutes, he wrote his most popular song, "No One Ever Cared for Me Like Jesus." George Beverly Shea and many others have recorded it. The chorus says, "No one ever cared for me like Jesus, there's no other friend so kind as He; No one else could take the sin and darkness from me, Oh how much He cared for me."

God does care for His people. All human life is sacred, and His people need to protect the dignity of life. We need to care for people, and we need to be cared for by others. When we know God cares for us, we can give and receive care from others. From conception to the grave, it is about caring.

February 2014

Healthy Marriages and Compatibility

It is generally acknowledged that Genesis 2:24 is the most important verse in the Bible on the subject of marriage. It does not, on first reading, say anything about compatibility. However, it is evident we cannot have a one-flesh relationship without it. Compatibility is essential for a godly and healthy marriage, but the key is in how we define it.

Compatibility does not necessarily mean being alike but having the ability to live together in harmony. The root of the word may also suggest the ability to suffer together. It implies things like sympathetic understanding and mutual stability.

Do men and women fall in love because they are compatible, or do they build compatibility because they love each other (are committed to each other)? The more a husband and wife please each other in marriage, the stronger the level of compatibility. According to John Gottman, the ratio of positive to negative exchanges in a marriage should be at least five to one. Pleasing behaviors build compatibility, and compatibility leads to happier and healthier marriages. To be compatible, we have to work at it.

Paul wrote in 1 Corinthians 7:33-34 that someone who is not married is concerned about pleasing the Lord, but someone who is married is concerned about the things of the world — how to please his or her mate. This is what I call the please principle. When we are committed to pleasing our mates, we build a more stable marital system and create compatibility, which, in turn, produces greater satisfaction in our marriage. A good marriage requires hard work based on true love.

Love in marriage is not a feeling, but a commitment to the other person. It is *agape*. Of course, affection, romance and acceptance are vitally important. Feelings follow love, just like behavior follows thought. But *agape* — the commitment to do what is best and right, and the willingness to do it in a way that is sacrificial and unconditional — is the foundation for a good marriage. Love in marriage is evidenced in how we value our mate. According to Ephesians 5:25, husbands are called to love their wives as Christ loved the church. We should love our wives enough to be willing to die for them. That is the greatest thing we can do, according to Jesus, in John 15:13: "Greater love has no one than this, that one lay down his life for his friends." If a husband can do the greatest thing for his wife — love her — then he can certainly do lesser things like listen to her, spend time with her, etc. Wives love (show value to) their husbands by responding submissively to that kind of love (Ephesians 5:22).

Love, or *agape*, is the fruit of God's Spirit in us. We are called to love our neighbor, love our enemy, love one another, and, most importantly, love God. We are counseled to love our mates.

Godly marriages — where two people love God and each other, please each other, like each other, and value each other — can be one of the strongest means for sharing the gospel of Christ in our culture. When people see the results of real love in our marriages, they are curious about it and attracted to it. Our compatibility can open doors of sharing and showing God's love and truth to others.

There are no perfect marriages because marriages are made up of imperfect men and women. However, love in marriage that is based on the love of God grows stronger and better as we move through the stages of life. Marriage, after all, is to be a picture of Christ and His church.

It is my hope and prayer that this issue of The Courier on love and marriage is a blessing to you.

MARCH 2014

THE GREAT COMMISSION IS NOT THE MAIN THING

This column may not be as controversial as the headline. In this issue of The Courier, we are focusing on "The State of the

Church." Our culture is rapidly becoming more secularized, and churches are not impacting the culture or reaching the percentage of people we once did. Some local churches are vibrant, but most are plateaued or declining — at least in terms of membership and attendance. The Southern Baptist Convention adopted a report from the Great Commission Resurgence Task Force, as did the South Carolina Baptist Convention from a similarly named task force.

The Great Commission is not the main thing, the only thing, or everything. It is an important, essential, and powerful commission for reaching the world with the gospel and discipling those who believe. However, it may not be the right place to start. The Great Commission must rest on the solid foundation of Jesus and the Great Commandment He gave us. Our purpose as followers of Jesus Christ is to glorify His name in everything we do. We are called to live with a comprehensive foundation of love — love that is rightly understood, married to truth, and active in living out the principles of Scripture.

In Matthew 22, a scholar in the Law asked Jesus which was the great commandment in the Law, or, as some translate it, what is the nature of the great commandment. Our Lord replied in verses 37-40, "And He said to him, 'You shall love the Lord your God with all your heart, and with all your soul, and with all your mind.' This is the great and foremost commandment. The second is like it, 'You shall love your neighbor as yourself.' On these two commandments depend the whole Law and the Prophets."

After hearing the Great Commandment and the second greatest, "Love your neighbor," a scholar of the Law asked Jesus, "Who is my neighbor?" Jesus replied with the story of the good Samaritan. Our neighbor is whoever God puts into the path of our life whose needs we can help meet. It is profound and yet simple: Love God with all our hearts, and love our neighbors as ourselves.

The Great Commandment is foundational to our lifestyle as Christians. The Great Commission grows from that foundation. All other commandments are summed up in these two. It is possible to focus on the Great Commission to the exclusion of the foundation that makes the Great Commission actually work.

In the days of the preacher-theologian G. Campbell Morgan, he observed that plenty of people attended church services yet did not love God. As with anything else in the Christian life, if we try to carry out any directive of Scripture without the motivation of genuine love, which comes from God, our efforts will fail to achieve God's intended design. Morgan wrote, "[God] can be loved only as He is known. He can be known only as He is obeyed." In John 14:21, Jesus said, "He who has My commandments and keeps them, it is he who loves Me." Two verses later, He said, "If anyone loves Me, he will keep My word." Obedience to the Word of God is at the core of what it means to love God. When we truly love God, we will obey His truth — including the Great Commission.

The Great Commission is vital. Today, we seem to be failing at carrying out that important commission. Could it be that we have failed to fully obey the Great Commandment upon which the Great Commission rests? None of us can claim perfection. That is not the question. Do we imperfect Christians love God and love that person who enters our circle of life?

There are so many facets to the modern church. Diversity among Southern Baptist churches is greater than it's ever been. We need each other. We need to disciple people all over the world. Most of all, we need to love God. The Great Commission is not the main thing, but it will be obeyed because of the main thing: love for God and for people!

June 2014

Is Biblical Preaching Relevant Today?

What helps Americans grow in their faith? Most who are reading this would probably include in their answer the study of God's Word and being involved in church. However, a recent survey by Barna Research dealt with that question. Church was not in the top 10. Over half of the respondents said attending church was "not too important" or "not important at all."

Across denominations and age groups, unchurched people were asked, "Why don't you attend church?" Forty percent said they "find God elsewhere," and 35 percent said, "Church is not relevant to me personally." When coupled with the recent report that skepticism toward the Bible continues to increase, the question arises, "Is biblical preaching relevant today?" My answer is, "Yes!"

All preaching or teaching is not necessarily biblical. But biblical preaching and teaching is not only relevant, it is also desperately needed. To grow as disciples of Christ, we need to read, study, understand and apply God's Word. We need preachers and teachers who will teach us God's truth. Jesus taught with authority, and faithful preachers and teachers of the Word today use His authority as their platform to communicate His truth.

Albert Mohler, president of Southern Baptist Theological

Seminary, wrote, "If there is a crisis in preaching, it is a crisis of confidence in the Word. If there is a road to recovery, it will be mapped by a return to biblical preaching."

Robert Smith, professor at Beeson Divinity School, in his book, "Doctrine That Dances," said that preaching is "the escorting of the hearers into the presence of God for the purpose of transformation."

We need good and godly teachers and preachers. Romans 10:14 asks, "How shall they hear without a preacher?" Paul exhorts Timothy (and all preachers and teachers) to "preach the Word; be ready in season, and out of season; reprove, rebuke, exhort, with great patience and instruction" (2 Timothy 4:2).

How can we interpret Barna's statistics in the light of Scripture's mandate to preach and teach the Word? It all depends on our perspective. Many years ago, a shoe salesman went to an undeveloped country. He stayed a few weeks but sold no shoes. He telegraphed the home office that he wanted to come home because "nobody wears shoes here." A few weeks later, a second salesman arrived at the same place. After a couple of months, he sent a telegram to the home office, "Please send shoes. Everybody here needs shoes!"

People need to hear the Word. Even in our post-Christian culture, people need to hear the Word. Today is not the time to give up in frustration but instead to give out the clear, plain teaching of God. Some will hear, and their lives will be forever changed. We are saved by grace through faith. Romans 10:17 says, "Faith comes from hearing, and hearing by the word of Christ."

During his tenure as president of Southeastern Baptist Theological Seminary, Paige Patterson preached during a chapel service at New Orleans Baptist Theological Seminary. He challenged those attending by saying, "Ladies and gentlemen, the people in the church you're going to serve, wherever you go, are in a state of confusion. What is needed to speak to the confusion of our people is a generation of preachers who are Bible-teaching preachers."

Preaching and teaching God's Word is relevant today. In fact, it may be the only thing that is eternally relevant in an age of irrelevance. For those of you teachers and preachers who study diligently, pray fervently, and communicate God's truth faithfully — be encouraged. What you do is relevant and greatly needed.

September 2014

Remember to Care

Jeffrey Baldwin was an innocent 5-year-old boy who died from septic shock and bacterial pneumonia caused by prolonged starvation. This happened while he was in the care of his grandmother and her common-law husband. Jeffrey's case has been called the worst case of child abuse in Canadian history.

His story is one of tragedy, abuse, neglect and disappointment. There is not enough space here to detail his complete story, but some things should be told because this little boy and the abuse he suffered need to be remembered. We need to remember to care for little children.

Elva Bottineau, his grandmother, had a background of child abuse, and yet the Catholic Children's Aid Society of Toronto did not check its owns files until after Jeffrey's death. She was paid by the government to take care of Jeffrey and his three siblings. She did not. He and his older sister were both neglected and mistreated, but his sister managed to survive because she was allowed to go to school, where she was provided food and drink. He was kept in a room that was, by the best descriptions, terrible. He was beaten and starved. When he died at age 5 (almost 6), he weighed 21 pounds — one pound less than he weighed at age 1.

When emergency personnel arrived at his house, they were shocked. Jeffrey's body was skin and bones. Bacteria covered his body, and fecal matter clogged his lungs. The little boy had no pulse and was not breathing. He was officially pronounced dead later, at the hospital. None of the six adults who lived in the house seemed to care. Toronto Fire Department captain Royal Bradley said, "No one shed any tears for that little guy — except for a lot of firemen and police officers."

Jeffrey died on Nov. 30, 2002. His grandparents were later charged with first-degree murder. Their trial began on Sept. 8, 2005. On April 6, 2006, they were both convicted of second-degree murder and given life sentences. After the grandmother had exhausted all her appeals, a coroner's inquest began on Sept. 9, 2013. Just recently, the coroner's office completed their work and presented 103 recommendations for improving the system in Canada that is supposed to care for children.

Part of the jury's conclusion at the coroner's inquest was the hope that a permanent memorial could be established for Jeffrey "to provide the important and ongoing public safety message that the protection of vulnerable children in Ontario is every citizen's responsibility."

A bench and a plaque had already been erected in Toronto's Greenwood Park. The plaque reads: "In remembrance of a forgotten child who lived his short life locked away in hungry darkness kept out of sight, out of mind, starved of love, joy, and kindness. But smile now, child, be free now, child. Your sweet face will live forever in our hearts, and we will remember to listen to small voices and watch for sorrow in their eyes."

A father of three in Toronto, Todd Boyce, heard about Jeffrey's case. He started a fund to enlist the services of famed Toronto sculptor Ruth Abernathy to create a bronze statue of Jeffrey in his Superman costume. Wearing his hero's costume seemed to bring him the most happiness in his otherwise painful life. Most of the contributions came in from around the world through the Internet. The goal was $25,000. In a few weeks the goal had been exceeded. Work began on the project so, as Boyce put it, "Jeffrey would not be forgotten." However, DC Comics refused to allow the logo of Superman to be used on the statue — until there was an enormous public backlash. They soon relented, and now the statue will be placed with the bench and plaque at Greenwood Park this fall.

Jeffrey Baldwin was an innocent child who was forgotten and abused. It seemed that his life fell through the cracks. At nearly every turn in his short life, people, agencies, relatives, etc., failed him. But though his death was tragic, it awakened multitudes in Canada to the plight of child abuse. Changes in the systems that deal with children are already underway.

In America, according to the Department of Health and Human Services, the leading type of child abuse is neglect. More than 1,600 children die each year from abuse and neglect in this country. Amazingly, 80.3 percent of the perpetrators of child abuse are parents. Biological parents abuse their children approximately 85-to-1 more often than adoptive parents.

Child abuse is a problem, and abortion is child abuse. The

win-win solution to abortion is adoption, especially since adoptive parents are much less likely to abuse their children than biological parents.

As Christians, we have the privilege to demonstrate the love of Christ for these little ones. We should teach them the gospel, but we also must be committed to protecting their health and lives. We will not be able to see them saved if we don't work to keep them alive.

Jesus cares about children. We all need to remember to care for children.

It is not only our duty and our ministry — these children are the future of our civilization.

In Mark 10, Jesus emphasized that we enter the kingdom like a child. The context in Mark is that children were being brought to Jesus for blessing, and the disciples rebuked the people for bringing them. Verse 16 says, "And He took them in His arms and began blessing them, laying His hand upon them." May we likewise serve as the hands of Jesus for blessing, and not for harm. Remember to care.

April 2015

Easter Is Personal

I like Easter more than Christmas! Both are special and essential, and while the birth of Jesus is certainly significant, the resurrection of Christ from the dead is the foundation of our faith as Christians. First Corinthians 15:17 says, "If Christ has not been raised, your faith is worthless; you are still in your sins." But the resurrection of Jesus changes everything for believers.

I am currently rereading "The Valley of Vision," a collection of prayers and meditations by the Puritans. In a chapter called "The Spirit's Work," the author writes: "Lead me to the cross and show me His wounds, the hateful nature of evil, the power of Satan; May I there see my sins as the nails that transfixed Him, the cords that bound Him, the thorns that tore Him, the sword that pierced Him."

My mind began to think of two words: "For me." The suffering, mockery, and ridicule that Jesus suffered were for me. The loneliness like no one has ever experienced was for me. His pain and suffering from the spear thrust into His side, the pummeling He endured from the hands of His executioners, and the crown of thorns pressed onto His head were all for me. The scourging that nearly took His life was for me. When He breathed His last painful breath on the cross and died, it was for me. God made Him who knew no sin to become sin on my behalf, that I might become the righteousness of God in Him (2 Corinthians 5:21).

He died for me so I could live forever with Him and for Him. The resurrection proved that God the Father had accepted forever the sacrifice of Jesus for sin. His birth, His life, and even His death on the cross awaited the confirmation given by the resurrection. It proved that Jesus is who He says He is, and that He accomplished what He came to do. For all of us who truly believe, the result is forgiveness, acceptance and purpose.

Ronnie Hinson and Mike Payne wrote a song that reflects the personal nature of what Jesus did for those of us who believe: "When He Was on the Cross, I Was on His Mind."

The late E.V. Hill once commented on the power of the resurrection in a sermon. "That first Easter is so far away," he said, "but

I am here with the proof." The reality of the resurrection is alive in those who are alive in the risen Savior. The resurrection can stand alone on its own merits, but the personal joy that comes from the new birth is indescribable.

The resurrection is personal. It is not simply about you and me. It is about God's glory. Our call is to glorify Him in whatever we do. There is rejoicing in heaven when a sinner comes to Christ. He is the resurrection and the life, and we are blessed through saving faith in Him.

I hope you will take time to meditate on what Christ did on the cross, why He did it and for whom He did it. Think about it personally with gratitude and praise — it was for you and me.

Have a blessed Resurrection Day celebration!

MAY 2015

THE GRAYING OF AMERICA AND WHAT IT MEANS

Robert Browning wrote a poem — actually, something more like a philosophical text — from the perspective of a 12th-century person, Rabbi Ben Ezra (also the title of the poem). He begins, "Grow old along with me! The best is yet to be, the last of life, for which the first was made; Our times are in His hand, who saith, 'A whole I planned, youth shows us half; trust God; see all; nor be afraid.'"

Growing old is a reality of life — if we are fortunate. How we deal with aging is a question of attitude and faith. Growing old has implications beyond who we are as individuals, though; it affects healthcare, the economy, the church, our family and more.

If we continue to live, old age (like death) is inevitable. America is growing older. The graying of this nation, sometimes referred to as the "silver tsunami," is upon us. The first baby boomers, the generation born between 1946 and 1964, began reaching retirement age in 2011. This group of 74.9 million has changed culture at every juncture of their life stages, and they will likely affect how we interpret "retirement."

The website Policy and Politics asked this question: "Is the graying of America an economic time bomb?" A 2014 Gallup Poll reported that only one-third of baby boomers ages 67-68 were still employed. The pollsters concluded that this indicates boomers are not staying in the work force longer than those before them. If this is true, a shrinking work force could spell trouble for America. Business Journal says there is an "impending talent vacuum" as boomers, while working longer, are still retiring at a steady pace. A 2014 Harris Poll shows that 74 percent of boomers are concerned about having enough money in retirement, while 86 percent say the country is facing a retirement crisis. Seventy-four percent of those surveyed said it was important for them to feel financially confident before they retire, and 70 percent expect to work in some capacity following retirement. Retirement, it appears, is going to be defined more as a stage of life than a time of ceasing all employment.

A subgroup in the boomer generation has been tabbed the "sandwich generation" because they are assisting both older children and aging parents. This means the boomer generation, which is sometimes referred to as the entitlement generation or the generation of great expectations, as a whole will be forced to deal with pressure and sacrifice unlike what they have previously known.

The cost for treating and caring for elders with dementia is growing. Alzheimer's care is projected to exceed $1 trillion annually. By 2025, one in 26 Americans is projected to live to age 100. The Council on Social Education says that 30 percent of people ages 65-74 and 45 percent of those 85 and over suffer some type of dementia.

By 2050, projections indicate that the number of people 65 and over will rise to 88 million, meaning that one in every five Americans will be 65 and over. The average amount a 65-year-old can anticipate in medical expenses during his or her golden years is $220,000.

The statistics and projections could go on and on. The point is, our nation is aging and entering a time of unprecedented challenge. The largest generation in American history — the millennial generation (age 18-34), at 75.3 million — faces even greater challenges, but they are not currently entering the retirement years. This generation is expected to peak at 81.1 million in 2036.

The church today needs older people teaching, mentoring and helping younger people as we move forward. First Timothy 5:1-3 gives us wisdom that can be applied to our time and our future: "Do not sharply rebuke an older man, but rather appeal to him as a father, to the younger men as brothers, the older women as mothers, and younger women as sisters, all in purity. Honor widows who are widows indeed."

The time in which we live is the best time to live because it is the time God has ordained for us. A change is coming in America, and this country is more disconnected from Christ and the church than at any time in our history. Our population is aging. Christians are getting older, but we can and should be wiser and more useful in serving God and others. We can and should encourage, listen to, and help disciple younger Christians who are not just the future of the church but part of the health and vitality of the church today.

David wrote in Psalm 71:18: "Even when I am old and gray, O God, do not forsake me, until I declare Thy strength to this generation." Those of the baby boom generation have had a tendency to think of themselves above everything else. Now is certainly the time for this generation to think more of the next generation as they enter the "retirement years." Boomers can be such a force for godliness if they know God and are committed to making Him known to future generations. If they do, we all may be able to agree with Browning that "the best is yet to be."

June 2015

Encouraging One Another

Encouragement is such a powerful influence on a person's motivation. It takes about 10 positives to neutralize one negative, but we live in a world full of negativity. That translates into an even greater need to encourage one another.

In the book of Hebrews, the Jewish people who had professed faith in Christ experienced consequences from within their culture. Because of negative pressure — and even persecution — many of these believers were falling away from their profession of faith and returning to the law of the Old Covenant. Even those who did not fall away were likely feeling the temptation to turn away from openly following Christ. Some of them habitually neglected the gathering of Christians, which can be an initial step in falling away from the faith — and even into apostasy.

Hebrews 10:25 says, "Not forsaking our own assembling together, as is the habit of some, but encouraging one another, and all the more, as you see the day drawing near." Some translations use the word "exhorting one another" in this verse, but the force of encouraging is present also in the word exhort.

Our denomination faces challenges. Easily, more than half of our churches are declining or plateaued. Pastors feel the pressure and pain of this reality in their lives and families. Too often, a church seems determined to die rather than grow — because it is easier to die. A pastor might have solid training, a disciple-making commitment and good leadership skills and still find himself in a position where the church is stuck in a plateaued position or plunging into a downward spiral. In these situations, many pastors become discouraged. Yet what they need is encouragement. God seems to spell success "f-a-i-t-h-f-u-l." In fact, He requires His stewards to be faithful. As followers of Jesus, we may not always be successful by the world's standards, but we can always be faithful to Christ and His Word. Faithful pastors need the encouragement and the committed help of the congregation if a declining or plateaued church is able to grow again and become spiritually healthy.

Church members in a stalled or dying church also need encouragement. That is why Hebrews 10:25 is so relevant for our times. Encouragement cannot take place in isolation but should occur in the gathering of believers. In fact, the encouragement in our churches should be so genuine and God-motivated that it inspires the members to become greater witnesses outside the walls of the church building.

The failure to encourage one another can be devastating to a church. We need God, and we need each other. Someone once said that encouragement "is to a group of people what wind is to a sailboat — it moves you forward."

When we encourage someone, we literally inspire that person with hope, confidence and courage. It is likely that more than half of those who read this column are pastors or church members in a declining or plateaued church. What can you do? To borrow from a counseling technique: Accept what is real, make realistic goals, and work toward the goals. An unknown writer said a bend in the road "is not the end of the road — unless you fail to make the turn."

The Holman Christian Standard translation in Hebrews 3:13 says, "Encourage each other daily." Encouraging other believers does not mean we compromise truth, overlook sinful practices, or embrace a pop psychology that is going nowhere eternally. Rather, it means we love God and the family of God enough to support them in the journey of faith. At the end of our time, our goal is to hear from Jesus, "Well done, good and faithful servant."

Today, we need to give and receive encouragement more than ever.

Freedom-Fed Patriotism

In his essay, "The Czar's Soliloquy," Mark Twain wrote, "True patriotism, the only rational patriotism, is loyalty to the nation all the time, loyalty to the government when it deserves it." As we approach our patriotic holiday on July 4, the idea of patriotism is displayed and discussed in our society. But what is patriotism, and is it okay to be patriotic and a Christian simultaneously?

Elton Trueblood said of Abraham Lincoln, "His patriotism was saved from idolatry by the overwhelming sense of the sovereignty of God." In Paul's sermon on Mars Hill in Acts 17:26, he emphasized that God "made from one, every nation of mankind to live on all the face of the earth, having determined their appointed times, and the boundaries of their habitation." The nation we live in is an appointment from a sovereign and almighty God. This realization keeps patriotism in perspective and keeps God's gracious providence central in our thinking.

Patriotism means devotion to one's country, loyalty to our country, or defense of our country. It can be emotional and expressive, or quiet and contemplative, but it always has the concept of devotion coupled with an appreciative attitude toward the nation. While patriotism can be displayed through flags, songs, ceremonies, tributes, gatherings, etc., the best kind of patriotism is rooted in devotion, respect and thankfulness.

The kind of patriotic spirit that is most vibrant is the one that reflects the foundation and ideals of freedom. Our founding fathers reflected a biblical influence that guided their thinking, resulting in documents committed to freedom — like the Constitution, the Declaration of Independence, and the Bill of Rights. They emphasized that we have certain inalienable rights like life, liberty and the pursuit of happiness, which are not bestowed to us by government but by our Creator.

Lawrence W. Reed, president of the Foundation for Economic Education, said, "Freedom — understanding it, living it, teaching it, and supporting those who are educating others about its principles. That, my fellow Americans, is what patriotism should mean to each of us."

John F. Kennedy, America's 35th president, said, "Let every nation know, whether it wishes us well or ill, that we shall pay any price, bear any burden, meet any hardship, support any friend, oppose any foe to assure the survival and the success of liberty."

At the core of real patriotism, whether it is found in our nation or in other nations, is the idea of freedom. Throughout American history, the concept of freedom has been a defining hallmark. Our nation is not perfect, but it is our nation. It is still a land of freedom. In times past, we adapted and changed in order to correct a course leading us away from freedom. Some of our freedoms, especially religious liberty, are being threatened today like never before.

During America's early years, the French writer Alexis de Tocqueville said, "The greatness of America lies not in being more enlightened than any other nation, but rather in her ability to repair her faults." That is a powerful observation. I hope and pray that statement is proven true in our lifetime.

"God Bless America" is a song, a slice of political rhetoric and a heartfelt desire. That's what most of us Christians want for our country. Because of the issues we face in this country and a culture that is becoming more and more hostile to the Christian faith, perhaps we should alter that slogan slightly. Maybe our prayer should be, "God Change America" — so that we can more completely be the land of the free, the home of the brave, and a lighthouse for the one true God.

September 2015

Domestic Abuse Is Sin

Domestic abuse is a sin, and it is a growing problem in this country — even within the professing church.

Lifeway Christian Resources last year reported that 42 percent of Protestant pastors rarely, or never, speak about domestic violence in sermons. Russell Moore, president of the Ethics and Religious

Liberty Commission of the Southern Baptist Convention, says we "must teach from our pulpits, our Sunday school classes, and our Vacation Bible Schools that women are to be cherished, honored and protected by men." He emphasizes that we must "explicitly tell the women in our congregations that a man who hits you has surrendered his headship."

In a recent Christianity Today article, "The Silent Epidemic," writer Corrie Cuter noted that the American College of Obstetricians and Gynecologists reports between 3 and 4 million women are beaten in their homes every year. Retired detective Don Stewart, who handled domestic violence cases for 25 years, said that 25 percent of Christian couples experience at least one episode of physical abuse within their marriage.

Some are calling domestic abuse an epidemic in this country. While this deviant behavior is often infused with anger, the chief motivators are power and control. Usually, a man — using fear, intimidation, threats and even acts of abuse (physical, emotional, sexual) — tries to force compliance with his will on another person.

In Malachi 2:16, a parallelism occurs where a man who divorces his wife commits violence against her. Gary Thomas, author of "Sacred Marriage," wrote, "Malachi 2:16 is sometimes used to cement the opposite of God's intent: keeping a woman in a dangerous home." He adds: "The church should hate domestic violence as much as it hates divorce. It should support women caught in domestic violence as much as it offers divorce recovery programs."

Throughout history, women have been abused by men. While men are sometimes abused, the numbers cannot compare to abused women. It is disgusting for a professing Christian male to abuse his wife — or any woman — in any way. Physically, he may be able to do it because he is stronger, but 1 Peter 3:7 warns husbands to "live with your wives in an understanding way, as with a weaker vessel, since she is a woman; and grant her honor as a fellow heir of the grace of life, so that your prayers may not be hindered." Any man who says he walks with Christ and beats his wife is simply a liar. Men, in general, are physically stronger than women, but that should never be used as a bullying tactic to intimidate, control, manipulate or hurt someone.

Some people have attempted to connect a wife's submission to her husband as the basis for continuing abuse. In Ephesians 5:21 a general principle is given: "Be subject to one another in the fear of Christ." Christians should be submissive to one another. From that overall relational setting, verse 22 says wives should be "subject to their own husbands, as to the Lord." The principle of submission is specifically applied and addressed to wives, not husbands. Submission is a voluntary choice or act by the wife and cannot be made for her by her husband. Submission is something that cannot be coerced.

Wives are also called to respect their husbands (Ephesians 5:33), and husbands are commanded to love their wives as Christ loved the Church. Christ died for the Church! The command is for husbands to love their wives with a love that is willing to die for their wives. In John 15:13, Jesus said, "Greater love has no one than this, that one lay down his life for his friends." If a husband is committed to doing the greatest thing (that is, to die for his wife), he can certainly do lesser things, like listen to his wife, respect her, value her, provide for her and protect her. As James Montgomery Boice said, "No good woman will struggle hard against a man who is willing to die for her."

Any man who demands of his wife or tries to force her to submit to him has missed the point and is entering into the realm of abuse.

Domestic abuse is a sin, and the church needs to work diligently to teach people the truth about caring for one another. The second greatest commandment is "love your neighbor," and our mate is our number-one neighbor.

October 2015

Ministering to Addicts

Ministering to addicts can be frustrating. Those who seek to bring godly counsel and loving help to those caught in an addictive bond are to be commended, encouraged and supported.

For the past 18 years, I have served in a volunteer capacity as the counselor for Home with a Heart, a residential Christian rehab ministry for men. My weekly job is to teach a class on marriage, eat supper with the men, offer any counsel they may need and provide any other service within my limited capabilities.

Home with a Heart was founded in 1993. Alex Richey became the director in 2000, just a couple of years after he graduated from the program himself. What started with one building has grown into a 29-acre campus that includes two dormitories, a chapel, a commercial kitchen, a dining hall, a laundry building, a director's residence, five thrift stores, and a halfway house off campus. Approximately 50 volunteer ministers and lay people come to teach classes and serve in various ways each year.

Since its inception, 3,400 men have come through the program, and about 2,000 have made professions of faith. "I have probably baptized 800 men since I have been here," said Alex.

Most of the men complete the program and go on to lead lives of sobriety, with many becoming active leaders in local churches. What is the secret to the success of this ministry? Alex is quick to answer: "It's Jesus. We are a faith-based ministry, and Jesus is first in everything we do. He is the real hope and solution."

Unlike secular programs whose success rate is much lower, Home with a Heart daily brings the teachings of Scripture into the lives of addicts. Recently, one of the presidential candidates talked about the problem of addiction in America and offered a solution that would cost about $10 billion. At Home with a Heart, the mission statement is "providing rehabilitation and hope at no charge to men seeking freedom from the bondage of alcohol and drugs through Jesus Christ one day at a time." You would not find that purpose or strategy statement in any government-sponsored program. Life-change is the answer, not simply money. Lives are being changed at Home with a Heart. Jesus Christ is the focus, and His Word is foundational to everything that is presented. I have been privileged to be a part of that.

Local churches provide music and preaching for Sunday evening services in the chapel. The men attend various local churches together on Sunday mornings. The home has two camp-meeting-style revivals each year and various classes each day for the men. There is a fish fry and gospel singing most Friday evenings. Each month, the group also visits a local church with a Celebrate Recovery ministry.

The men work in the thrift stores, drive, load and unload the trucks, prepare the meals, and labor at many other tasks on campus that include tending to the cows, chickens and pigs.

Since men who enter the home incur no financial cost, support comes from grocery store donations, gifts from churches and individuals, and income from the thrift stores. About 75 percent of church support comes from Baptist churches.

Addiction is a growing problem in this country. Home with a Heart maintains a waiting list of people wanting to enroll. With an estimated 23 million addicts in America and only 10 percent of them seeking help, this is a problem that will be with us for some time. Another estimate is that 52 million people age 12 and over have abused prescription drugs, including 25 percent of teenagers.

Some men do not graduate from the home's program. Some relapse. Some have died. I have spoken at funerals where a drug overdose or alcohol poisoning was the mitigating factor in their deaths. It is heartbreaking to see families torn apart and children hurt because of substance abuse. But it is so gratifying to see families put back together and children given a better hope for life.

Occasionally I will encounter graduates of the home somewhere, and they are always quick to speak to me, often telling me how the home and my class helped them. There is no financial incentive for me. What I do on campus and in counseling the men after they graduate is free. As Alex shared with me years ago, "Your benefits for doing this are out of this world." He is right, but the joy of seeing Christ change people is a benefit of infinite value — and I get to see that many times a year.

APRIL 2016

JESUS IS SALVATION — ANYTHING ELSE IS COUNTERFEIT

The salvation we have by God's grace through faith in Jesus Christ is supernatural, but it is not merely something we add to our lives along with many other things — it is Jesus.

It begins with the new birth, continues as we grow in holiness, and culminates in the time of our glorification with Him. Salvation is not what we do, but what He has done for us and who He is in us (John 1:12-13). When we are saved, we surrender to Him. We belong to Him.

There is no lasting or redeeming relationship with God except through Jesus Christ (John 14:6, Acts 4:12). Jesus' name helps define the purpose of His coming: to pay the penalty of sin by dying on the cross (Matthew 1:21, 1 Peter 2:24, Luke 19:10). When the Philippian jailer asked Paul what he must do to be saved, the apostle replied: "Believe in the Lord Jesus."

God uses His Word to teach us who we are (lost, dead in our trespasses and sins — Ephesians 2:1, Romans 3:23) and show us His solution to our dilemma (John 5:24). How are we saved? Ephesians 2:8-9 says: "For by grace you have been saved through faith; and that not of yourselves, it is the gift of God; not as a result of works, that no one should boast." We are saved from damnation, hell, and the wrath of a holy God. As Herbert Lockyer noted: "Salvation offers emancipation from the bondage of sin and all its eternal consequences." We are saved to glorify God, obey His Word, do the good works He has prepared for us to do, and grow in holiness. We can love God and love our neighbor because He lives in us.

Jesus saves. It is God's work in our lives — and never some work of the flesh — that we may assume justifies us before Him. When we are saved, we are justified (declared righteous in Christ) by God Himself. We have a new standing before Him, and we have the presence of the Holy Spirit in us to guide, teach, convict, comfort and help us.

When I was 13, Preston Garrett led me to faith in Christ in my home. He used John 3:16 as he explained the plan of salvation to me. I knelt on my knees and trusted Christ as my Savior. I was saved. But salvation has three tenses. We are saved, we are being saved, and we will be saved.

After I began serving as a pastor, I wrote a booklet that I used to help Christians witness. It was based on John 3:16. Rev. Garrett preached at my ordination service. I remember fondly when he pointed his finger at me during that service and said, "Boy, you get on the trail and bark for Jesus!"

Today, I have one of Rev. Garrett's Bibles, given to me by his widow before her death. I am so grateful that he was faithful to present the Gospel to me. He is in heaven today, but I know he would be the first to say he was only a tool in God's hands.

Jesus is Savior and Lord. Salvation may seem to have some mystery, and even complexity, in all its dimensions, but the good news is that it is real. Eternal life is not just forever-existence, it is Christ Jesus living in us through the person of the Holy Spirit.

There is a tendency among professing Christians to substitute a cultural religion for a genuine relationship with Christ. Salvation is a relationship with Christ, and anything else is a counterfeit. As we travel through life, we make mistakes, fall short and sin. Yet, if He is our Savior, we can be secure. In Him, we are loved, accepted, forgiven, and so much more. Heaven is a reality we will experience because He is our Savior.

Because we are saved, we can, and we should, share the Gospel of our Savior with others. Born-again people are part of God's family who want the family to grow.

From beginning to end, our call is to glorify God in whatever we do. We can never repay him, but we can daily surrender our lives in obedience and service to Him. He is worthy, and His Spirit in us gives us lasting worth.

Together we can praise God for His glorious salvation!

MAY 2016

THE PRIVILEGE OF HAVING A GOOD MOTHER

My granddaughter, Gray, and I spend time with my mom.

May 8 is Mother's Day. It had many precursors in American history before Anna Jarvis created it in 1908 and worked to make it a national holiday in 1914. The idea of Mother's Day creates an array of responses ranging from maudlin sentimentality to outright hatred. It is lamented as nothing more than a commercial scheme to make money and lauded as a special day to remember, honor and give tribute to mothers.

The Bible in Exodus 20:12 and Ephesians 6:2 admonishes us to honor our fathers and mothers. That certainly means more than just one day, but it does not exclude a day we set aside to especially honor and recognize mothers.

My mother will turn 86 in September. I have lots of memories of her that touch my heart with gratitude. She was kind, patient, caring, giving, comforting, encouraging and involved. When I was an elementary school kid, she paid special attention to my grooming and made sure I was neatly dressed before school each day. When she came to pick us up from school, I am sure she was shocked at the transformation that had taken place in just a few hours!

She loved holidays and family. She was faithful in church, even when I did embarrassing things like lock the preacher and his class in a room during Vacation Bible School. She was present for every significant event in my life. Her love and devotion were obvious.

She has lived with Alzheimer's, often referred to as the "disease of the long goodbye," for more than eight years. She still speaks, but most of her words are not really words. When I visit her, she does not know who I am. She has osteoarthritis and osteoporosis and has fallen twice, resulting in a broken hip and broken shoulder. She cannot walk or feed herself. Her hands are fixed in a clutched position.

Before the Alzheimer's had worsened, I talked with her about her relationship with Jesus Christ. She assured me she was born again. Even though I have a voice that resembles a sick bullfrog, I began to sing "Amazing Grace." To my surprise she joined in and sang it with me. Even though I was unaware of it at the time, my wife recorded the whole scene on her cell phone.

Recently, one of her caretakers at the facility where she lives asked me if she had three children. Apparently, she had been talking about her three children. She gave birth to three children, but I am the only survivor. However, that question stimulated my thoughts and memories, and I believe that she carried sadness in her heart over the two children who are buried next to my dad. She wanted a family with several children, but her doctor advised her not to have any more children. I am confident that she will be reunited with all her children one day.

Until that time, it is my desire to honor my mother as the Scripture teaches us to do. I miss my mother's love of holidays and birthdays, and her enjoyment of her grandchildren. She is unaware she has great-grandchildren. My mother was the inspiration behind the book I wrote, "Worry: The Silent Killer." When I was worried about something, she would tell me not to worry because most of the things we worry about never happen. As it turns out, she was right.

This Mother's Day, remember the mother you had or spend some time with the mother you still have. I hope my mother has been honored by at least some of my life as I have tried to follow Christ Jesus. She deserves it, and she will always have a special place in my heart. Looking back over a lifetime, I am so grateful for the mother God gave me.

I hope you have a blessed Mother's Day.

July 2016

True Champions for Christ

Bobby Richardson signing autographs.

In 1974, I was working as a young sportswriter for the Anderson Independent and was given the assignment to do a full-page feature on Bobby Richardson, head coach of the University of South Carolina's baseball team. It was my first big story, and I enjoyed interviewing the former New York Yankee second baseman.

The Gamecocks were preparing for their first-ever NCAA baseball tournament appearance. Richardson had built a mediocre program into a national contender in four years. His strong and public commitment to Christ distinguished him from most other coaches.

During Richardson's tenure at Carolina, Ed Young, then pastor of Columbia's First Baptist Church, was chaplain of the baseball team.

My wife and I recently spent a day with Bobby and Betsy Richardson. They continue to live busy lives. The phone rings every few minutes, more than 50 pieces of mail come every week with requests for autographs, etc., and they are continually asked to speak or appear at various functions. It is amazing. He retired from the Yankees at age 31 and will turn 81 in August. To say they are still active would be an understatement.

We began our day with Betsy leading us in prayer. Bobby and I attended a men's monthly luncheon in Sumter, where a speaker shared the Word of God and various prayer requests were received. People in his hometown call him Coach, but Betsy continues to call him Robert. She pointed out that, over the years, "Robert treated everyone the same. He would give time to anybody and has always been a giving person." Her husband, in turn, spoke in glowing terms of Betsy's role as a wife, mother, grandmother and great-grandmother. "Most of all," he said, "she is a faithful witness to our Lord."

He won the last of his five Gold Glove awards in 1965. It wasn't until 2010 that a Yankees second baseman won that award again.

He has personally led many people to faith in Christ, including many of his Yankee teammates. He has spoken at the funeral services of many teammates, including Roger Maris, Mickey Mantle, Steve Hamilton (who named his son after Richardson and accepted Christ in their home), Enos Slaughter, Bill Schrown, Clete Boyer, manager Ralph Houk, Bob Turley, and others. He also spoke at the funeral services of former Gamecock standouts Hank Small and Gary Hancock.

He had a relatively brief but exceptional professional career in

Major League Baseball and used that platform to be a bold witness for Christ. He said, "I always tried to live my life in a way that I hoped would cause my teammates to be drawn to my Savior." However, he said he "shuddered" that some of his teammates may have gotten the wrong impression. He and shortstop Tony Kubek were roommates on the road and were nicknamed the "milkshake twins" because of their clean living. Mickey Mantle once told Betsy he could not live as good as Bobby. Richardson says he wanted his teammates to know that "the source of my strength was Jesus, not a religion or self-discipline."

Bobby and Betsy do not hold themselves up as a perfect couple, and they freely share about their struggles. However, they have remained faithful to God and each other for over 60 years.

Richardson concluded his book, "Impact Player," with these words: "When accounts of my life are written, I hope two things will be said of me. First, that I played baseball in a way that made my team better. Second, and more important, that I lived my life in a way that drew others to my Savior."

I began my article about Bobby Richardson in 1974 with these words: "In short, he is a winner." Forty-two years later, I would not change that assessment but simply add that he is "a man of proven consistency and loyal faithfulness." He has fought the good fight of faith, and his race is not finished yet. Bobby and Betsy are both true champions for Christ.

August 2016

The Confederate Flag Is Out, But Is Racial Reconciliation In?

Scripture teaches us that it is good for brothers to dwell together in unity. Different races should be able, by God's grace, to live with mutual respect for each other. I don't see racial reconciliation as the goal, but the product of God's people walking in obedience to His Word.

National Baptist Convention president Jerry Young said during the June Southern Baptist Convention meeting in St. Louis that the problem was the church not being what God has called the church to be. "The problem is contaminated salt, concealed light, whereby we do not express the love of Christ nor extend His light," he said.

Perhaps the biggest story coming out of the SBC's annual meeting was a resolution against the Confederate flag. The resolution itself was strengthened through an amendment made by James Merritt, former convention president. His impassioned speech roused many of the messengers. His amendment and the resolution, as amended, both passed overwhelmingly. Merritt wrote on his blog following the vote: "Our nation, in some ways, has come full circle from Ferguson to Charleston to St. Louis, [but] many still harbor racist attitudes. It has become a barrier to even considering the Christian faith among many African-Americans. But, as a Christian, I know that every Confederate flag in the world is not worth one human soul of any race."

The resolution made headlines across the country. In the body of the resolution, South Carolina's leaders and the leaders of the South Carolina Baptist Convention were praised for influencing our state to remove the Confederate flag from the Statehouse following the Emanuel 9 murders. Then, SCBC president Tommy Kelley and interim executive director-treasurer Richard Harris issued a statement calling for the removal of the flag. All seven SCBC institution presidents supported removing the flag.

On July 6, 2015, the South Carolina Senate voted 37-3 to remove the flag from the Statehouse grounds, and the House followed suit in a 94-20 vote. Gov. Nikki Haley signed the bill banishing the flag from the Capitol grounds, and on July 10 it was taken down in a public ceremony and placed in the Confederate Relic Room and Military Museum about a mile from the Capitol building.

Former governors Dick Riley, David Beasley and Jim Hodges joined Gov. Haley at the bill signing. Beasley, a Southern Baptist who lost his re-election bid to Hodges — in part because of his support for removing the flag — was there to watch the flag-removal ceremony. He said that he always believed he would live to see the flag taken down one day. "I didn't know when, and obviously God's own time is not my timing, but it was worth the wait," he said.

The Southern Baptist Convention, following the action of South Carolina, has now passed a resolution urging Southern Baptists to refrain from flying the battle flag. For South Carolina and for the SBC, the disavowal of the flag was a big issue.

But now a bigger question remains. Will these actions motivate and inspire us to build the kind of healthy racial reconciliation that can only come through the strength of God and the wisdom of His Word? Let's pray that the love of God dwelling inside us will be greater than the prejudices that all of us have felt at one time or another.

When we seek first His kingdom, we will work toward racial acceptance, and we will judge no one by the color of his or her skin.

When that happens, it will touch our world in an unforgettable way as people witness the work of God's transforming grace in us. Let us pray that genuine racial reconciliation will happen in our denomination, our state, and our nation — not because our goal is racial reconciliation, but because of our obedience to God, which will bring racial reconciliation and so much more.

January 2017

Adoption ... It's Personal

Ben and Papa

Adoption is more than just an alternative to abortion. For my family and me, it is personal.

Anne and I are the proud grandparents of three of the greatest blessings God has ever given us. One of our grandchildren is adopted, and because January is Sanctity of Human Life emphasis, I want to share some things about him.

Our grandson is all boy. His entrance into our daughter's and son-in-law's lives as a newborn baby was nothing short of miraculous. My daughter, like her dad, is sure about her convictions. To say we are pro-life would be an understatement. She volunteers at a crisis pregnancy center and is a strong advocate for the unborn and for adoption. Her husband likewise is a staunch supporter of life and adoption. He is currently serving on the board of a crisis pregnancy center.

But our grandson is a special gift from God. Early in his life, some people said, "My goodness! He looks like his papa!" I found myself filling up with what I hope was sanctified pride. I hope and pray that God gives me the opportunity to see him grow up, trust Christ as his Savior and experience the great adoption that every child of God shares.

He could have easily been aborted, and that would have been a tragedy. He is alive and active today because his birth mother chose life. His parents are thankful every day for that decision.

My grandson and I are buddies. One day I called him "Hotshot." After telling me that we don't use that word, he later told me to call him Hotshot and even told other people (including his parents) to call him Hotshot. A couple of weeks later, he asked me to call him Hotshot Lightyear (after Buzz Lightyear).

I love to ask him, "Whose boy are you?" When he replies,

"Papa's," I swell up with that sanctified pride. I ask all my grandkids the same question, and they all answer, "Papa's." By the way, their parents don't mind. Neither does my wife, because she asks them, "Whose sweet boy (or girl) are you?" and they reply, "Mimi's."

In a Baptist Press article from last January, Pat Ennis, who was adopted as an infant, wrote that she "looked like the perfect blend of my mother and father. As others commented on the likeness, my parents smiled inwardly knowing that it was their heavenly Father who had chosen the custom matching of their adopted daughter."

What a wonderful thought!

Abortion has been a blight on the moral fabric of this nation. So many lives are damaged through abortion, while so many lives are blessed through adoption.

The sanctity of human life is dear to the heart of our family. It is not just a moral decision, a political position, or some abstract principle. He is a little boy, and we dearly love him. Adoption is not just an alternative to abortion, it is a life-saving experience full of blessings.

February 2017

The Blessing of Friendship

W. Ray Partain, one of the best friends I have ever known, died suddenly after a massive heart attack in December.

Ray became a very successful businessman after he "retired" from his regular job. When he started his income tax and bookkeeping business around 40 years ago, he dedicated his business to Christ.

Throughout the years, he has shown me again and again what a true friend is.

Baltasar Gracian said, "To find one real friend in a lifetime is good fortune; to keep him is a blessing." Ray was a real friend, a committed Christian, and a benevolent servant. He tithed for almost all of his working life. He was the greatest encourager I have ever known. He never failed to call me on my birthday. He is the only person who has ever done our income taxes. He and his wife, Nancy, drove a long distance to attend graduation services when I received my doctor of ministry degree.

I spoke at his funeral, wearing a bow tie in his memory. Ray started wearing bow ties many years ago, which became part of his visible identity. But he was so much more.

When he was a boy, he had a problem with stuttering. At least once a week, he would go to the country store in his community, where grown men gathered to gossip each day. They delighted at hearing Ray stutter, and they laughed and ridiculed him for it. But, like most everything else in his life, Ray overcame his stuttering and became a public speaker — teaching Sunday school, serving as a Gideon and being a toastmaster.

He cared about people and would often help those in need with money, food or other gifts.

During my first pastorate, he was a deacon. I remember the day his 17-year-old son was killed in an automobile accident. Ray was at the Georgia Baptist Assembly attending a music conference when he was contacted to come home. The house was filled with people when he arrived. Immediately upon receiving the news of his firstborn's passing, he asked me and another pastor to come to the bedroom with him and Nancy to pray. Ray prayed, asking God for help and for strength to be a good witness, while thanking Him for being God.

During the visitation at the funeral home, many people came. One lady approached Ray with the intention to provide comfort until she broke down in tears in front of him. He took a handkerchief from his pocket, gave it to her with a hug and assured her that everything was going to be okay. He was a powerful witness during that painful time in his life.

A couple of years after his son's death, Ray and I went to the prison in Columbia to visit a young man. On our return, a highway patrolman pulled me over for speeding. He asked me to come back to his car, and we talked. When he told me he was only going to give me a warning ticket, I was relieved, but I felt I should share the plan of salvation with him. The trooper turned off his radio, bowed his head and prayed to receive Christ. When I returned to my car, I discovered that Ray had adjusted the rearview mirror to see what was transpiring and was praying the whole time. "I knew you were going to witness to him," he said, "so I started praying."

There are so many stories and memories of my dear friend that I will cherish. He is in heaven today, and I grieve, but his impact on my life will live on. In 2015, I wrote a little book called "You Can Live Until You Die," in which I related the stories of several people who did not give up on life until their last breath. Ray was one of the people I interviewed. When I asked him about retirement, he said, "Retirement is not in my future." At the time of his death, he was in a new office, still doing bookkeeping and income tax returns, but also working to expand his business by obtaining his insurance license.

He was a blessed man and a blessing to many others. He once

told me, "I can get emotional talking about how the Lord has blessed me."

W. Ray Partain was 79, and he truly lived until he died. Proverbs 18:24 says, "A man of many friends comes to ruin, but there is a friend who sticks closer than a brother."

Someone has noted that real friends are the siblings we never had. Ray, then, was my brother. While I will dearly miss him, I am so glad for the friendship God gave us.

An Irish proverb says, "A good friend is like a four-leaf clover — hard to find and lucky to have." Amen, and amen.

April 2017

Blessed Resurrection Day!

Resurrection Day falls on April 16 this year. Popularly known as Easter, this is a Sunday set aside to especially rejoice and celebrate the resurrection of our Savior and Lord Jesus Christ. We can rejoice every day, but it is good to have a day to remember and meditate on history's greatest event.

It is also the time of year when secular media usually produces some type of documentary in an attempt to disprove the resurrection.

What if there is no resurrection? Paul answers that question in 1 Corinthians 15. If there is no resurrection, then:

— Christ has not been raised from the dead (verses 13, 16)

— Preaching means nothing (verse 14)

— Faith in Christ is empty (verse 14)

— The apostles were liars (verse 15)

— Christians are lost (verse 17)

— Dead believers are in hell (verse 18)

— Christians are simple fools who should be pitied (verse 19)

But the Bible is crystal clear: Christ rose from the dead and He lives today! When Jesus rose from the dead, He proved that everything He said, did, promised and lived was true.

After our Lord's dead and mutilated body was taken down from the cross, He was buried in a tomb. Then His followers waited.

Imagine what those three days were like! He promised He would rise from the dead, but anyone could say that. He said He came to be the sacrifice for sin, but anyone could say that.

The proof would come three days following His death in the most momentous and powerful moment in human history. Jesus rose from the dead! His sacrifice and offering for our sins had been accepted by The Father. The sin debt had been paid in full, and people who trust in Him could enter into a forever relationship with Him.

First Corinthians 15:3-4 says, "I delivered to you as of first importance what I also received, that Christ died for our sins according to the Scriptures, and that He was buried, and that He was raised on the third day according to the Scriptures."

I appreciate the lines of the song that says, "Because He lives, I can face tomorrow." I never fail to be moved when I read the account in the Gospels on His resurrection day: "He is not here, for He has risen."

Elitists, secularists, and postmodernists may mount attacks against the resurrection, but they cannot remove it from history. The Christian faith is the only faith where our Founder loved us enough to die in our place, experience the wrath of God for us, pay the price for our alienation, and then demonstrate to the world His accomplishment by conquering death for us.

One day, every knee will bow and every tongue will confess that Jesus is Lord. Until then, we may be harassed, persecuted, even tortured, but we can never be without Him who is the resurrection and the life.

The empty tomb says more than "What an accomplishment!" It shouts for anyone to hear: "What a Savior!" I hope you and yours will enjoy a blessed Resurrection Day.

MAY 2017

THE IMPORTANCE OF BIBLICAL TRUTH

Some younger Southern Baptist ministers are asking the right question. Their question is not "What will work?" but rather "What is biblical?" Pragmatism is not unimportant, but it cannot be the foundation for our ministries and missions. What is practical can be chosen over what is biblical truth, but not without regrettable spiritual results.

International Mission Board president David Platt recently said, "The Bible is where the IMB must start in all of our missiology." He went on to say that missionaries must reflect the life-change that "is wrought by the gospel." So should every born-again person.

As our postmodern culture becomes increasingly more doubtful and even hostile to biblical truth, we can anticipate God's people either compromising in order to get along and perhaps gather more people into our church buildings, or choosing to faithfully and uncompromisingly live our lives on biblical truth. In postmodern thought, nothing is certain, and if someone believes in absolutes, they are regarded as arrogant or ignorant. Biblical faith and postmodernism cannot coexist.

Charles Spurgeon withdrew from the Baptist Union of Great Britain in 1887 because he was convinced the group was moving deeper and deeper into liberalism. He believed that universalism and Unitarianism could grow in the absence of strong biblical doctrine. Thirty-one likeminded ministers, along with Spurgeon, reaffirmed the "inspiration, authority and sufficiency of Scripture" as they withdrew from the Baptist Union. He faced intense opposition for holding fast to his convictions.

Spurgeon, pastor of the Metropolitan Tabernacle in London, one of the largest congregations of its time with a weekly attendance of 6,000, did not believe big numbers in worship services necessarily meant true worship was taking place. For him, a large church did not always mean a biblically sound church. "It could mean that it is swollen," he said. Spurgeon felt the churches of his time were like the church of Laodicea, as recorded in Revelation 3. Many contemporary pastors and Bible students have also embraced the concept that many of the churches of our age are like the church in Laodicea.

In Martin Luther's time, the Catholic church had fallen into many unbiblical practices, such selling indulgences. He was convicted that salvation was by grace alone, through faith alone, in Christ alone. Luther spoke out against the biblical errors of his church and became a major figure in the Protestant Reformation. When he was called to recant his writings by church officials, he stated, "My conscience is captive to the Word of God ... I cannot and will not recant." As a practical matter, he could have chosen to go along with those he knew were wrong and avoid the conflict that disagreeing brought.

He did not. He chose to stand on the truth of God.

The Southern Baptist Convention went through the Conservative Resurgence in the 1970s-1990s, yet today we are still facing the temptation to exalt pragmatism over biblical doctrine. Albert Mohler, president of Southern Baptist Theological Seminary, wrote: "Our identity must be more theological than tribal. Will we demonstrate theological and moral courage in the face of stiffening cultural opposition?" That is a vital question that has only one right answer.

Over the past few years, we have been a denomination in decline. We are still one of the largest denominations in the country and, in my opinion, potentially one of the best to reach people worldwide. Yet the panic to get more people into the church gathering has tempted us to compromise basic biblical truth. Southern Baptists, who have been known as "people of the book" (the Bible), have in some cases relied on practicality at the expense of biblical doctrine.

Success has come to be defined in terms of cultural meaning rather than biblical truth. Too often we have encouraged people, in regard to Scripture, to ask, "What does that mean to me?" instead of "What does that mean?" Scripture is objective truth from God. How we feel about that truth is not as significant as the fact that it is truth.

Compromise is wise in some things, but it is counterproductive, and even destructive, when it comes to Bible doctrine. While we may disagree on points of interpretation, we must be rock-steady in our commitment that what we interpret comes from God's infallible truth.

Whatever we do, we must do it from the foundation of God's truth. Otherwise, we open ourselves to the uncertainty and instability of subjective reasoning.

June 2017

Even in Retirement, Be Sure to Live Until You Die

Retirement is a word that is not going to be deleted from our dictionaries, but what that time period means should be, and is being, redefined. People can retire and do basically nothing, or they can stay active and accomplish much.

Dr. George Burch was an internationally known heart surgeon who taught at Tulane University School of Medicine. He is attributed with the saying: "The quickest way to the end is to retire and do nothing. Every human being must keep an interest in life to keep living." He remained a full-time faculty member until his death at age 75 in 1986.

The only record of retirement in the Bible is mentioned in Numbers 8:24-26. The Levites were required to retire at the age of 50, but they could continue to serve in less physically demanding roles. They were allowed to assist their brothers in the tent of meeting and fulfill any obligations they had made.

Thomas Haggai — former pastor, motivational speaker, president/CEO and chairman of the board at the International Grocers Association — has had a long and illustrious career and continues to work at age 85. Every morning, he prays, "Lord, don't let me die until I am dead!" He says, "I feel like you have to remain flexible enough to respond affirmatively to the opportunities that come your way. Every day we must exercise mentally, physically and spiritually in order to be ready for these opportunities."

Living until we die is a major challenge for many in the

retirement years. Some grow weary, and others give up. Tragedy or debilitating health issues sideline others. Yet, even in unfavorable circumstances, we can live triumphantly. When Jesus promised abundant life to us, He did not put an age requirement on it. He did not limit it to circumstances but tied the experience of it to Himself.

A redefined experience of retirement would be refreshing — a time when we continue to remain as active as we can, serving God as faithfully as we can, and growing spiritually as much as we can. When we retire, we can retire "to" something instead of "from" something.

While age can bring with it wisdom, and youth can supply strength and energy, we must have the right focus in order to really live. That focus is Christ: seeking His kingdom and righteousness above everything else, forgetting what lies behind, and reaching forward as we take our next step in the journey of life.

Seniors may be in the fourth quarter of life, yet our focus should not be on the three quarters behind us, but on the quarter in which we are living. Mark Twain said, "Old age is a matter of the mind — if you don't mind, it doesn't matter." John Piper stated that reading the works of C.S. Lewis revealed to him that "newness is no virtue, and oldness is no vice. Nothing is inferior for being old, and nothing is valuable for being modern."

The face of Kentucky Fried Chicken, Harland Sanders, became a millionaire after age 65 and a Christian after age 75. As Yogi Berra said, "It ain't over till it's over!"

Better yet, Jesus said, "No one, after putting his hand to the plow and looking back, is fit for the kingdom of God" (Luke 9:62).

Keep plowing. Stay focused. Live until you die.

November 2017

The Thanksgiving Lady

I enjoy fall and, particularly, Thanksgiving. This holiday has increasingly become a precursor to Christmas, but it is a great national celebration in its own right with a solid Christian origin.

Around 50 million people will travel at least 50 miles to have a Thanksgiving Day meal with friends and/or loved ones. Approximately 88 percent of Americans will eat turkey as part of their meal. It is a time, in spite of the turmoil and tension in our nation, to simply be thankful for the blessings of God. That was the original intent, and it is still viable today.

Many of us may call to mind the 1621 gathering of 50 Pilgrims with 90 Wampanoag tribesmen, a harvest celebration that lasted three days. Whether we mark that date as the beginning of our Thanksgiving tradition, or other dates predating or following it, the journey of Thanksgiving through the years still rests on the foundation of thanks to God for His blessings.

Sarah Josepha Buell Hale was a persistent and determined woman who worked diligently to make Thanksgiving a legal, permanent and national holiday. She spent 36 years campaigning, writing letters, lobbying, and using her influence as editor of the leading lady's magazine of the time to push for a national Thanksgiving Day holiday. Finally, in 1863, President Abraham Lincoln issued a Thanksgiving Day proclamation for the nation. He followed Sarah Hale's advice and chose the fourth Thursday in November for the holiday.

She had previously written: "Thanksgiving Day is the national pledge of Christian faith in God, acknowledging him as the dispenser of blessings." Following Lincoln's second proclamation in 1864, she wrote: "It is the peculiar happiness of Thanksgiving Day that nothing political mingles in its observance. It is in its very nature a religious and domestic holiday."

Presidential proclamations continued through the years. The fourth Thursday of November wasn't always the day for the holiday, although that was the day Sarah promoted. In 1871, she started a new crusade in an effort to persuade Congress to enact a law making the fourth Thursday in November a national holiday. She continued writing Thanksgiving Day editorials until 1875. It wasn't until her latter years that she discovered that President George Washington had issued a Thanksgiving Day proclamation in 1789 — for the last week in November. She passed away at age 91 in 1879.

In 1941, Congress voted to make Thanksgiving Day a permanent national holiday to occur each year on the fourth Thursday of November. President Franklin D. Roosevelt signed the bill on Nov. 26.

Sarah Hale was married for nine years when her husband died of a stroke. At age 34, she was left to raise three sons and two daughters, ages 2 weeks to 7 years. She worked as a writer and became the first female editor of a periodical for women called Ladies Magazine, which later merged with another magazine to become Lady's Book. Along the way, she wrote an enduring nursery rhyme, "Mary Had a Little Lamb."

Hale was a Christian who adamantly opposed slavery and tirelessly worked for educational opportunities for women. She died before her dream of a national Thanksgiving holiday was law, but her diligence prepared the way for it.

Thanksgiving Day is a great holiday, and giving thanks is a biblical command. Psalm 91:1 says: "I will give thanks to the Lord with all my heart." We can all thank God for the example of Sarah Hale and gratefully praise God for simply being our great God.

Have a blessed Thanksgiving Day!

DECEMBER 2017

THE SEASON WE CALL CHRISTMAS

Lottie Moon

The Christmas season is upon us again, and with it comes a unique mixture of sacred, secular, wholesome, sinful, pagan and Christian opportunities and obstacles. Christmas is a time of year that affects almost all of us in one way or another.

Following the Civil War, Southern Baptists, who had not been particularly involved with Christmas, began to embrace the holiday. Churches became more and more Christmas-friendly, as evidenced in the singing, plays, nativity scenes, fellowships, musical presentations, children's events, and various opportunities to serve and witness.

A major influence in the Southern Baptist Convention's embrace of the Christmas holiday was Lottie Moon, missionary to China. In 1887, she wrote a letter to the Foreign Mission Journal, proposing a season of prayer and giving among our churches for international missions. She suggested the week before Christmas.

She wrote: "Is not the festive season, when families and friends exchange gifts in memory of the one Gift laid on the altar of the world for the redemption of the human race, the most appropriate time to consecrate a portion from abounding riches … to send forth the good tidings of great joy into all the world?"

Stephen Wilson writes that for many years "the centerpiece of Southern Baptist holiday activities remained the promotion of the Lottie Moon Christmas offering for the support of foreign missions."

Lottie Moon was not accepted when she first arrived in China, but as she became more and more like the Chinese, she was more widely accepted and trusted. One thing that helped her connect with the Chinese was the teacakes, or cookies, she made for them.

Maybe someone would like to offer "Lottie Moon cookies" to a gathering this Christmas and use it to open the door for some gospel conversations. Here is the adapted recipe: 2 cups flour, ½ cup butter, 1 heaping cup of sugar, 1 well-beaten egg, and 1 tablespoon of cream. Mix the ingredients thoroughly into dough. Roll the dough on a flat surface sprinkled with flour and cut the dough with a round cookie cutter. Place on a buttered or nonstick cooking sheet and bake for 475 degrees for approximately five minutes.

Lottie's original recipe for "Plain Tea Cakes" was 3 teacups of sugar, 1 teacup of butter, 1 teacup of sour milk, 4 pints of flour, 3 eggs well beaten, and ½ teaspoon of soda. Her advice was to "bake in a quick oven."

The Lottie Moon Christmas Offering is a strong tradition in the SBC. The International Mission Board's statement regarding the offering is that "100 percent of gifts to the Lottie Moon Christmas Offering fund IMB missionaries who are making disciples and multiplying churches among unreached people and places."

If we really want to send more money to international mission work, we do not necessarily need to reorganize the convention or even designate money to the International Mission Board. Give through your local church to the Cooperative Program. Then, simply increase the amount you give to the Lottie Moon Christmas Offering. This year, the national goal is $160 million, which goes to support 5,000 missionaries and their work across the globe.

While the Week of Prayer for International Missions is not the week before Christmas, as Lottie Moon originally requested, it is still observed. This year it is Dec. 4-11.

This is a Christmas tradition that we can totally support. It is an opportunity to demonstrate that Southern Baptists are better together. To reach this year's goal will require SBC churches to give with fervor, and even sacrifice. When you make your Christmas list and wrap your Christmas packages, be sure your gift to Lottie Moon stands out. My wife and I are committed to giving our largest Christmas gift to the Lottie Moon Offering.

In our country, Christmas is a merging of secular winter festivals and Christmas traditions. For Southern Baptists, the hallmark of our celebrations used to be the Lottie Moon Offering. Wouldn't it be great if we again made it the hallmark of our Christmas season?

The early church did not celebrate the birth of Jesus, and we are pretty sure Jesus was not born on Dec. 25. But Jesus was born, died on the cross, and was raised from the dead. Today He lives. The Christmas season, which is usually characterized by the giving of gifts, can be a great opportunity to give a monetary gift that can have eternal impact. It is a time we can celebrate the birth of Jesus and honor Him by giving — and giving sacrificially — to the Lottie Moon Christmas Offering.

February 2018

Living in 'Post-Truth' Times

Barna Research recently reported that in our "post-truth" climate, reality is relative and "even the facts are open to interpretation." Barna went on to report that "one third of Americans say they trust nobody, only their own instincts, when consuming news."

It seems that postmodernism has given birth to post-truth. Barna asked this question in its survey: "Is moral truth absolute?" The answer: "Twenty-one percent never thought about it; thirty-five percent said absolute; forty-four percent said relative."

American philosopher Daniel Dennett called postmodernism an evil school of thought. He said that postmodernists "are responsible for the intellectual fact that made it respectable to be cynical about truth and facts."

Modernism had its greatest influence following World War I. The emphasis was on rejecting conventional style in literature and departing from classical and traditional forms. Science grew to be the answer for mysteries, not Scripture. After World War II, postmodernism, a reaction against modernism, began to grow and develop. It was a way of thinking and writing that is unscientific, irrational and, typically, illogical. The idea in postmodernism is that ultimate truth cannot really exist. Postmodernism is a pasting together of many different ideas and concepts that often conflict with and contradict each other.

In 2016, the Oxford Dictionaries International Word of the Year was "post-truth." The word itself can be traced back to at least 1992, but it flashed onto the world stage in 2016 when its usage increased by 2,000 percent from 2015. In a nutshell, a post-truth culture states that all claims to truth are relative to the particular person making them. That means one person's "truth" is as good as that of someone else who may have the opposite position. The idea of objective, verifiable reality and actuality is gone.

The evidence of a post-truth society are things like fake news, alternative facts, subjective interpretations, disinformation and misinformation. The concept of truth becomes increasingly irrelevant or virtually meaningless. The conclusion is that a person has a right to believe whatever he or she wants to believe without evidence or conformity to truth. In that type of atmosphere, lying is normalized, moral absolutes don't exist, and God becomes a subjective idea rather than the Holy God revealed in Scripture.

How can we live in a post-truth climate? As believers, our trust is in the God who is real and whose Word is objectively and positively true. We obey His teachings, and we guard our hearts against becoming like the post-truth culture around us. This is a time in which we must be wise as serpents and gentle as doves. To have an impact on people who are living out the post-truth narrative, we need courage and grace. We cannot be like them in order to win them. Rather, we must be genuinely different from them, but care enough to live and speak the truth before them. We do not need to judge or condemn them — they are condemned already because they have not believed in the name of the one true Savior. We can connect the lost to a biblical understanding of Jesus and His truth without being offended by their questions.

A post-truth system has always, in different lands and in various ways, existed. It has never been this comprehensive and widespread before. If we know the truth, as Christ said, it will set us free — and enable us to do the right thing. He said His Word is truth. He said He is the Truth.

Living in post-truth times is a challenge, but it is also the time in which we live. Our calling to be witnesses of Christ and His gospel has not changed. God has the power to save anybody out of any environment. He has chosen to use His people as His tools in this gathering process. We must, therefore, be those who speak the truth in love.

In May 2017, Pew Research noted that Americans have "low trust" in social media but trust family and friends for information more than anything else. People we know will likely listen to the message of Scripture we give them. God may use that as a means of grace to save people in this post-truth culture.

Knowing, living and sharing the truth, person to person, in a post-truth era can be a blessing beyond our expectations. Don't give up on truth, because it comes from God, and He never changes!

March 2018

Counting Your Blessings

On Tuesday, Jan. 16, there was an electrical fire in the basement of the offices of The Courier. Our staff had just finished the February issue and had to vacate the building. Duke Energy disconnected the power, and it will not be reconnected until we make repairs and also bring our wiring up to the new codes for the city of Greenville.

The staff has been divided into four different working locations while we wait for the work to be completed. This has been an inconvenience, but we have been blessed with the technology to continue our work and provide the March issue of The Courier on time.

As I thought about this experience, I began to think about blessings, those beneficial and favorable things God does for His people. No one was injured in the fire. Our building was not destroyed, and we have insurance. We have been able to continue to work and communicate with each other through various means, including getting together in one place for weekly staff meetings.

Jeremiah 7:7 and Proverbs 16:20 say: "Blessed is the one who trusts in the Lord." It is a blessing to be a child of God, and God blesses His children in so many ways. Eric Hoffer says the "hardest arithmetic to master is that which enables us to count our blessings." Charles Dickens wrote: "Reflect upon your present blessings — of which every man has many — not on your past misfortunes, of which all men have some."

The idea of counting blessings may seem novel, but I can testify that it is so refreshing and encouraging when you actually do it.

Laura Story's song, "Blessings," and "Thank You Lord for Your Blessings on Me," written by James Easter and his sons, are encouraging words about simply being thankful for God's blessings even when they are disguised. Circumstances may change, but God never does. He is always and forever the same loving, righteous, faithful God. He causes all things to work together for good to those love Him and are called according to His purpose (Romans 8:28).

As I thought about blessings, it became personal: my new-birth experience, the call to ministry, our marriage, our children and their mates, our grandchildren, and the time I had a near-death experience while on a mission trip to Honduras (not to mention being helped by an angel!).

There are so many more blessings I could easily list. As my thoughts on blessings continued, my heart was joyfully and deeply moved. Our oldest daughter, Becky, and her husband, Timothy, adopted a newborn more than five years ago. He has been a great blessing, along with our other two grandchildren (whose parents are Katy and Jonathan). Becky was told by her doctors that she likely could not have children. She had exhausted every means available, including surgery. At 37, her family was set — until recently, when she discovered she was pregnant! Her doctor went over her medical records, pointing out her history, then paused and said, "And you are pregnant. Wow!" Becky shared with the nurse that some people had been praying for her to get pregnant. The nurse replied, "That makes the hair on my neck stand up!"

The baby is due in June, and all the tests have been perfect. What a blessing! Needless to say, we are all excited and thankful.

As I studied and contemplated the subject of blessings, it became evident to me that God wants us to love Him as the blesser more than we love the blessings He gives us. However, I am convinced He wants us to recognize, appreciate and be thankful for all His blessings. Counting our blessings is a good and healthy practice. I believe that old song, "Count your Blessings" by Johnson Oatman Jr., published in 1897, is on target: "When upon life's billows you are tempest-tossed, when you are discouraged, thinking all is lost, count your many blessings, name them one by one, and it will surprise you what the Lord has done." The last stanza says: "Do not be discouraged, God is over all; count your many blessings, angels will attend, help and comfort give you to your journey's end."

Amen! Counting our blessings is not a waste of time, but a reminder of God's faithfulness.

April 2018

What a Providential Time for Gospel Conversations

Billy Graham died Feb. 21 and was buried on March 2. During that time, the world was exposed to the word "gospel" in an unprecedented way. Tributes to the great evangelist came from people in all walks of life. News organizations and social media sites played video clips of the respected man of God delivering his powerful gospel message. His death could actually reach more people with the gospel than his life!

Combined with the Easter season that is upon us, Billy Graham's death opens the door for doing more than just talking about gospel conversations — it is the prime time to be having gospel conversations. The opportunity is wide open because millions of people have heard about Billy Graham's death and seen video of messages he delivered more than 50 years ago and throughout his life. With all the attention on "America's pastor" and the worldwide celebration of Easter, what an opportune time this is to share the gospel of Jesus Christ. For disciples of Christ, the death of a prominent evangelical leader, combined with the perennial emphasis on Easter, present a ripe time for sharing His good news.

People were touched by the integrity, goodness and morality of Billy Graham. His death affected people around the world. Perhaps some hearts have been softened, and some minds are now willing to at least consider the message he preached. On the heels of Graham's death comes the greatest event in the history of the world, the bedrock of the Christian faith: the resurrection of Jesus Christ.

Many Christians shared nostalgic memories or moving tributes to Billy Graham, the man. But what would Graham himself want at this juncture in time? I believe he would want people to take advantage of this opportune moment to talk about the message behind the man. No doubt, many people who were touched by his death do not understand what the new birth is all about. They appreciate the man, and they are impressed by the fact that he preached to more people than anyone in history, but they may not have a genuine relationship with God through faith in Jesus Christ. What better time than now to talk about what he preached about?

It can be as simple as sharing John 3:16. It can start with, "I guess you heard about Billy Graham," and continue with, "Did you know he preached basically the same message for 60 years?" Then, a conversation about the death of a great man leads to a conversation about the greatest man — who not only died for our sins but rose from the dead! I believe many people have been prepared during this time to hear — with more than just a passing interest — the gospel message.

Samson was a mighty man of God who succumbed to temptation and fell into disgrace. As a prisoner of the wicked Philistines, he was mocked and blinded. As they gathered to offer sacrifice to their god Dagon and boasted that "our god has given Samson our enemy into our hands," Samson began to pray.

About 3,000 people, including the Philistine elites, had gathered to watch and mock their former antagonist. According to Judges 17, God gave Samson strength, and Samson pulled the main pillars of the building down, giving his own life and taking the lives of the Philistines. Judges 17:30 says, "So the dead whom he killed at his death were more than those whom he killed in his life." In a similar way, wouldn't it be great if God's people, even in their grief, captured this moment in history and carried forward the mission of our beloved Billy Graham?

One professor, evaluating Graham's sermons, noted, "Regardless of what he preached, he always headed to the cross." Let us use this open door God has given us — in the death of perhaps the greatest evangelist in history — to reach the multitudes Graham so passionately desired to reach. How remarkable that his death can become a tipping point for many to investigate the power and meaning of Christ's resurrection. Though they are grateful for God's man — Billy Graham — they may come to faith through the abiding witness of God's eternal redeemer — Jesus Christ.

Hebrews 9:27 says, "It is appointed to men once to die." The timing of Billy Graham's death was no accident; it was appointed by God. Someone once said, "With God, time is irrelevant, but timing is everything." Touch someone with the gospel during these few days of tremendous opportunity — while mourning the death of a great man and yet celebrating the resurrection of God's Son, whom that great man loved. The timing is providential.

August 2018

Detours on the Roman Road

For most of my 37 years as a pastor, I primarily used the "Roman Road" when witnessing to lost people (Romans 3:23, 3:10, 5:12, 6:23, 5:8, 10:9-13). It did not always lead to an immediate profession of faith, and there were often detours and surprises. I want to share a few of those experiences with you.

Early in my ministry, we would go on "visitation" to the homes of people we thought were not Christians. Often, we knocked on doors randomly. On one of my first such surprise visits, my visitation partner was a UPS worker. We encountered a big, growling dog in the neighborhood. I was afraid, but he was experienced with situations like these. He slowly led us away, calmly talking to the dog as he jingled the keys in his pocket. We did not see anyone saved that night except ourselves!

On another occasion, I was in a man's home sharing with him the Roman Road. I asked him if he would like to trust Christ as his Savior. He said yes, and I helped him pray. Then I said, "Now, if you were to die tonight, where would you spend eternity?" He replied, "I don't know." I then repeated the Roman Road again, prayed with him, and asked him the same question. He said again,

"I don't know." I said, "Why did you pray and confess Christ as your personal Savior?" He said, "I don't know. I thought that is what you wanted me to do!"

One night I was witnessing to a man who was home keeping his preschool-age son while his wife was out. I tried to move down the Roman Road with him, but his son had a little plastic baseball bat that especially made me nervous after he hit me in the head with it. The man did not make a profession of faith, but we did pray. (My eyes were open.)

Another man I visited was a professing Christian, looking for a church home. We went over the Roman Road together, just to be sure. After some conversation, I shared with him that I was going dove hunting with some friends in a few days. He said, "I don't know about that, pastor. You know that the words 'In God We Trust' are engraved on the breastbone of a dove!" I thought he was kidding, but he wasn't. I politely excused myself, realizing he probably needed more professional help than I could provide at that time in my life.

At McCall RA Camp one summer, I was the camp pastor. Several of us prayed during the week for a great moving of God's Spirit. On decision night, as I extended the invitation, 100 boys made decisions. Just a few years ago, I was invited to speak at a Christmas event designed to help needy families with their Christmas gifts. When the invitation was given, 103 people made decisions at the altar. Those were the two largest evangelistic responses I experienced in my ministry.

One special experience stands out in my mind. It was not a time when many responded to the gospel, but when one person, through the process of time, believed. It goes back to the time when I was a youth minister, around 44 years ago.

We were preparing to leave the church for a fun night of miniature golf and McDonald's. All the teens knew they were to bring their own money for the trip. As I looked around before we departed, I noticed a girl who seemed isolated and unhappy. I knew her situation, so I asked her privately if she was OK. She said, "I know we were supposed to bring money, but I don't have any." I knew she did not have anyone who could give her any money. I told her it was all right, and I discreetly gave her some money. She enjoyed herself immensely that night.

The next Sunday, she wanted me to see her new Bible. (She did not have one previously.) She said, "I was able to buy this with the money left over from the youth trip." I did have the privilege to share the Roman Road with her, and she trusted Christ and was baptized.

Time passed, and I moved on to new fields of ministry. Many years later, when I was preaching at a church revival meeting in Anderson, this same girl attended one night — this time with her daughter. After the service, she said, "Do you remember me?" I did. She reminded me about the Bible she bought as a teenager with the money I had given her, and she told me she was active in her church serving Christ.

That was one of best investments I have ever made!

Whatever plan we use, we all have the opportunity to share the gospel with lost people. There may be some detours and surprises, but there will also be memorable blessings!

September 2018

What a Great Name for a Pastor

Wes Church and his family

What a great name for a pastor: Church. Wes Church, that is. He is the new senior pastor at First Baptist Church of Columbia, having served on staff for 16 years at the church. Even though he is stepping into a new position, he has a history of faithful ministry in the 200-year-old historic church.

In 1988, Kenny and Cindy Church, along with sons Ken and Wes, moved to Spartanburg. A few months later they joined Roebuck Baptist Church, where I was the pastor. I had the privilege of baptizing 9-year-old Wes and his older brother, Ken, together. I was blessed to watch Wes grow in his faith for a short time before I accepted the pastorate of another church in 1994. In 1995, Tim Williams became the pastor at Roebuck, where he continues to serve.

Tim said, "Wes was bright, talented, and, best of all, committed to Jesus Christ. I am confident Wes will be a great pastor that God will use to lead one of our most significant and historic congregations to new heights."

It is always encouraging to watch someone mature from a child to an adult and make an impact serving the Lord. Wes comes from a strong Christian family. He attended Columbia First Baptist while he was a student at the University of South Carolina and was interested in the college ministry there following graduation. However, he was already committed to a summer job and did not feel he could apply for the position. His mother encouraged him to inquire about the intern position. He accepted the position of college intern in July 2002. A few months later, he became the college minister. Sixteen years later, he was unanimously called as pastor. She said, "I have always prayed that my boys would be in the center of God's will. I am very grateful that God has brought Wes to this place. God has used him to minister to others throughout his life, and I am excited to see God continue to use him as the senior pastor of First Baptist Church, Columbia."

Some may think it is surprising that a soon-to-be 39-year-old's first pastorate would be at First Baptist of Columbia. However, after interviewing several people who know him well, a consistent response emerged: "I am not at all surprised by this." David Satterwhite, minister of music at Roebuck for over 30 years, said, "When Wes was very young, I could tell God had great plans for him. He was a natural leader."

This issue of The Courier focuses on discipleship, and Wes is committed to evangelism and discipleship. He believes being a disciple and helping others to become disciples are what it is all about. He said, "I have great hope that First Baptist Church will grow as a congregation, filled with fully devoted followers of Christ, who love God, love people, and make disciples." He believes that "the best place for true life-change and discipleship to occur is within the context of a small group." He understands the importance of discipleship and brings to his position experience in directing the discipleship strategy of the church for the past seven years.

First Baptist is a church rich in history. The first president of the Southern Baptist Convention was also the church's first pastor, William Bullein Johnson. The chapel is named for one of the founding fathers of Southern Baptist Theological Seminary, James Petigru Boyce. It is one of the larger churches in the South Carolina Baptist Convention and now occupies one entire city block in the state capital.

While Wes is in a new position, he is not new to the congregation. The love between pastor and people is evident. He possesses unique gifts, an engaging personality, a thirst for excellence, an unwavering commitment to Christ and His church, and a love for the people.

I believe Columbia First Baptist Church has made a wise decision, and I will prayerfully and expectantly watch as God, working through Wes, accomplishes His purpose and glorifies His name in the midlands and beyond.

December 2018

A Christmas Eve Near the Moon

1969 USPS commemorative stamp featuring NASA's "Earthrise" photo from Apollo 8 mission.

On Christmas Eve in 1968, Apollo 8 astronauts Frank Borman, Jim Lovell and Bill Anders orbited the moon 10 times. During that historic day, they photographed the earth rising above the moon's horizon. "Earthrise" would become one of the most iconic images of our planet.

During their Christmas Eve lunar orbit, they read the first 10 verses of Genesis 1, which was broadcast worldwide to the largest TV audience in history up to that time. The first verse says, "In the beginning God created the heavens and the earth." That verse seemed to take on a unique and memorable experience as it was read by the men who had traveled farther into space than any human beings before them.

On Christmas morning, the astronauts reached for their dehydrated meals, which they admitted were not a delight to eat. When they opened the food compartment, they were pleasantly surprised to discover three foil packages wrapped with green and red ribbon. Inside was real turkey, dressing, gravy and cranberry sauce, along with some small gifts from their wives. Borman said it was the best meal of the flight.

As they reignited their engine and left lunar orbit on Christmas day on their way back to earth, Lovell, to the delight of children everywhere, said, "Please be informed: There is a Santa Claus." The crew landed safely on earth Dec. 27.

In 1969, the U.S. Postal Service issued a commemorative stamp featuring the "Earthrise" photo with the words: "In the beginning God … ." It was a different time in the 1960s, but the shift to a more secular mindset was already developing in the culture. Madalyn Murray O'Hair filed a lawsuit against NASA for the astronauts' reading of the Genesis passage during the mission. In 1970, the Supreme Court dismissed her case.

Things have changed greatly since then. In fact, according to Pew Research, fewer Americans — even those who are Christians — hold to four essential truths presented in the Bible: the virgin birth of Jesus, the account of Jesus being laid in a manger, the wise men being guided by a star to Jesus and bringing expensive gifts, and the angelic birth announcement of Jesus to shepherds.

We are a much more secular society than we were then. The Christian faith is not welcomed today as it was back then. But we still have the same God and the freedom to worship and serve Him, particularly during the Christmas season.

John 1:1 says, "In the beginning was the Word and the Word was with God, and the Word was God." John 1:14 adds, "And the Word became flesh and dwelt among us."

Christmas is a time for believers to celebrate the incarnation — God becoming a man. Our celebrations should at least be as special as the Apollo 8 experience.

We at The Courier hope your Christmas will be special and meaningful to you this year. In adapting the words of James Lovell, please be informed: There is a Jesus Christ, and He is the living Lord!

January 2019

Alzheimer's Didn't Win

My mom with her granddaughters, Katy, Becky and Cindy.

On Thursday, Nov. 29, around midnight, surrounded by the people she loved most on this earth, my mother breathed her last breath. For over 12 years she struggled with Alzheimer's, coupled with osteoarthritis and osteoporosis. Her battle was over, and even though this sinister and devastating disease viciously attacked her body and brain, it did not win.

In Matthew 10:28, Jesus said, "Do not fear those who kill the body, but are unable to kill the soul." Alzheimer's is a fearful disease, but it cannot touch the soul of a child of God.

For several years I struggled with how to pray for my mother. I came to the place where I simply asked God, among other things, to give my mother peace in her soul. When she breathed her last breath, it was so serenely peaceful in that room. It was an unforgettable moment. She was gone, but Alzheimer's didn't win. In the end, it just opened the door to a better life. The Apostle Paul said that it was much better to depart and be with Christ, but he stayed on in this life for the sake of God's work and God's people.

My mother loved me unconditionally, and as I grew older — and, hopefully, wiser — I saw how exceptional that was. She was the inspiration behind a book I wrote on the subject of worry, and she left a good and godly imprint on my life.

Pain is never an easy road to travel, and it must be scary when you cannot remember the most important people and things in your life. But God has promised to always be with His people. I believe He was with her as she died. Some medical professionals refer to the time when a person begins the dying process as transitioning. I believe it is at this time that a believer experiences God's dying grace. I saw my prayers answered in the peaceful death of my mother. The atmosphere in the room seemed to change. In over 40 years of ministry, I have watched a handful of people die and have preached at many funerals. But this was my mother, and it was very different.

She was saved when I was a child. With limited memory, I do recall when she joined the church and was baptized. I also vaguely remember the graveside services for my younger brother and sister. She carried them to full term, but they died at, or just before, birth. There was a subtle sadness that she lived with after that, especially when she discovered she could not have other children. She really wanted a large family. But, when grandchildren came along, it seemed to inspire her to a new level.

My three daughters loved their grandmother, and she dearly loved them. They all wrote tributes to her. My wife, Anne, read them at the funeral, and I want to share some excerpts. Becky wrote, "She was a Titus 2 woman who taught us by example what was good so that we would be encouraged as young women to love our husbands and children and to be sensible, pure workers at home." Katy said, "She was a kind, generous, gracious and hard-working woman who lived a life of humility and put her trust in Jesus as her Lord." Cindy observed, "Never in my life did I doubt how much my grandparents loved me, and that is one of the greatest gifts I can imagine."

It should not be, but often is, that a mother-in-law and daughter-in-law do not get along very well. That was not the case with Anne and my mother. Anne said, "I could not have asked for a better mother-in-law. She loved me and welcomed me into her family. When Rudy and I disagreed, she always took my side. Now that's a good mother-in-law!"

When you watch someone struggle with Alzheimer's, you understand more personally a description that has captured the pain of that journey: the disease of the long goodbye. You watch your loved one lose their cognitive skills, memory and so much more. It is a disease that takes different courses in its victims. Someone once noted, "When you know one Alzheimer's patient, you know one Alzheimer's patient."

When death finally came to my mother, a grief I didn't anticipate rolled over me like a tidal wave. As much as I hate Alzheimer's, though, I know Alzheimer's did not win.

First Corinthians 15:55-57 says, "O death, where is your victory? O death where is your sting? The sting of death is sin, and the power of sin is the law; but thanks be to God, who gives us the victory through our Lord Jesus Christ."

My mother is with Jesus. She suffered and fought a good fight against a disease that takes no prisoners. While this disease is brutal, Alzheimer's did not win. The love of Jesus won big time for my mother.

MARCH 2019

IT'S MORE THAN ST. PATRICK'S DAY

March 17 is St. Patrick's Day, and while it is not a Baptist distinctive, it is a memorable day for my wife, Anne, and myself. I proposed to her on that day, and she accepted.

In Ireland, Patrick is regarded as a saint, although he was never canonized by the Catholic Church. He has been called the Apostle of Ireland because of his missionary work there in the fifth century.

St. Patrick's Day in America is marked by traditions different from those observed in Ireland. In America, we seem to think that cabbage and corned beef is the food we should eat on that day. However, in Ireland, the food consumed is a wide variety of meats, vegetables and desserts. In both countries, St. Patrick's Day is a secular time marked by parades, food, the wearing of green (the color of the shamrock), and drinking.

There is a legend that St. Patrick used the shamrock, a three-leafed clover, to explain to people the concept of the Trinity (using the three leaves and one stem as a symbol). The shamrock is the national flower of Ireland, and it (or a shamrock pin) is often worn on the holiday.

All of that is irrelevant and unimportant to my wife and me. St. Patrick's Day is special to us because it is our engagement day: March 17, 1977. Later that same year, on Aug. 19, we were married. It has been a great journey that began with both of us, even before we knew each other, praying to God for a mate and for direction in how to serve Him. I was pastoring my first church (and was serving as that young church's first pastor), and Anne was teaching high school math. God, in His providence, answered our prayers and brought us together. She has continued to be my helpmate and my rock.

A few weeks ago, I was diagnosed with a serious medical condition. It was news I did not want to hear. Neither did Anne. Again, we prayed and sought direction. She has been relentless in questioning doctors and following up to make sure we got test results back as soon as possible. Our 50th wedding anniversary is in 2027, and I hope and pray that I will be here to celebrate it with her.

March 17 is special for us — not because it is St. Patrick's Day, but because, on that day, we began a journey that continues to this day. Our nearly 42 years together have been graced with so many blessings. At the top of the list are three daughters, three sons-in-law, and four wonderful grandchildren. We have learned much together and, by God's grace, will continue to learn more about Him and love Him better until He calls us home.

Anne and I have pleasant thoughts when we think about St. Patrick's Day, because that's when a bond was established between us, and with God, and that bond has endured. When a life-threatening disease crosses your path, it gets your attention. It also compels you to focus more intently on the matchless God you know. That is where we are today.

St. Patrick's Day is something small, but God is amazingly large. He makes the impossible, possible. He alone deserves our worship and praise. March 17 is just another day on the calendar, but Anne and I will recognize it not as a holiday but will recall, with thankful hearts, the fact that God led us to each other.

All God's children share the same amazing comfort of His presence. He has promised us, "I will never desert you, nor forsake you" (Hebrews 13:5). As my speech professor in college used to remind us: "Today is the first day of the rest of your life!"

April 2019

Gratitude for God's Mercy

In our March issue, I mentioned a life-threatening disease I was facing. It was an aggressive carcinoma in the prostate. Radical surgery was performed on Feb. 21, and the results have been amazing!

I cannot capture in words my overwhelming sense of gratitude to God for His mercy. When the final pathology report was explained to my wife and me, tears flooded our eyes. The medical team was convinced they got all the cancer! As of this moment, no further treatment is planned.

So many people called, texted, visited and prayed. Churches, groups and individuals interceded for us before God's throne of grace. Of course, our family also prayed diligently. My sweet wife, in spite of my objections, did not leave my side except for the actual time I was in surgery.

While the recovery has been much longer than I expected, the opportunity to stay on this earth a while longer leaves Anne and me with the sense of being exceedingly blessed by the God who heals. As God allows, we look forward to serving Jesus, watching our grandchildren grow up, and celebrating our 50th wedding anniversary in a few years.

The surgeon said, "I believe we got lucky and caught this early." I was encouraged by his words, but deep in my heart I was made humbly aware of the touch of Jesus Christ and the sovereign power of Almighty God. I am thankful for skilled surgeons, caring nurses, committed support workers, and the prayers of family and friends. But the words of a dear friend and medical doctor sum it up for me: "God is the healer. We do not heal. We are simply the tools God often uses to heal."

The result could have been much different, and God would still be the same powerful and loving God. But, for this time in my life, God demonstrated to me on a deeply personal level His matchless grace, His ability to answer the prayers of His people, and His great wisdom to use whatever means He chooses to accomplish His purpose.

It is my delight to serve as editor of The Courier and to preach in the churches of our convention. The Courier is celebrating its 150th anniversary this year, and we are working to make it a memorable time. The first issue of The Working Christian, which later became The Baptist Courier, was published on July 1, 1869.

In our next issue, we will have the plans finalized for the celebration. Space will be limited for an anniversary dinner in June, but all our readers will be invited to attend as long as space is available.

Psalm 46:1 says, "God is our refuge and strength, a very present help in trouble." Psalm 9:1 says, "I will give thanks to the Lord with all my heart." Many years ago, a dear pastor friend used to say, "I just want to brag on Jesus!"

Me, too!

June 2019

The Power of Theology Is Applying It

Recently, my middle daughter shared with me that she and her husband were reading through Wayne Grudem's "Systematic Theology." I was impressed, to say the least! She said it was not difficult reading.

That conversation spurred me to think through the whole subject of theology. We might have a tendency to think of it as dull, difficult or boring. But good theology is very important if it is applied to life. Theology is more than just a grouping of topics or doctrines from Scripture. It is a perspective or worldview that enables us to see and interpret life more accurately. It organizes important truths in a way that helps us to better understand our Lord. Jesus said, "You shall know the truth and the truth shall make you free." Good theology that develops out of a belief in God's unerring Word will make a big difference in how we live — if we apply it to our daily lives.

In 1857, John Dagg published his "Manual of Theology." He stated that "to study theology for the purpose of gratifying curiosity is an abuse." We should study theology in order to become better servants of Christ.

In an interview, Grudem described systematic theology this way: "Take all the appropriate verses (of Scripture) to see what God wants us to believe about a specific topic. The Bible is internally consistent, not contradictory." He further points out that the danger in simply studying theology is that it can become nothing more than an intellectual activity. He said that after studying a topic, we should ask, "How does that apply to my life?"

John Frame, Grudem's mentor, pointed out that systematic theology is "the application of God's Word by persons to all areas of life." The goal of Bible study is to practice what we learn.

It is a consistent theme among the best theologians, from ancient times to the present era, that theology is designed not simply to inform us but to inspire us to live lives that obey God's truth and glorify God's Son.

The best way to interpret Scripture is with Scripture — comparing Scripture with Scripture. Good theology books do that, and a good personal theology seeks to live according to the Scripture.

Today, we can become somewhat confused by the different prefixes assigned to theology.

The two most prominent types of theology are biblical theology and systematic theology. Geerhardus Voss in "Biblical Theology" wrote in 1948, "Biblical theology is systematic and systematic theology is biblical. The Scriptures constitute the sole material from which the science of theology can deal."

It is possible to have a good theology or a bad theology. One good test to determine if what we believe is true is to test it with Scripture. As John MacArthur states, "The true test of doctrine is to drag that doctrine through every text in Scripture."

Theology simply means "the study of God." What we can know about God with certainty is found in Scripture. The Word of God is our base of authority for knowing God. Albert Einstein stated, "Intellectual growth should commence at birth and cease only at death." Our growth as Christians should begin with our new birth and continue throughout this life and beyond.

My daughter has inspired me. I think I will read Grudem's "Systematic Theology" this summer. Even though I have read several theology books and even taught theology classes, I have a long way to go. Our pilgrimage as followers of Christ is to learn His truth and live it. That is a never-ending process.

The real power of theology is not only knowing it but applying it.

September 2019

Remembering September 11

While focusing on the month of September for my column, I was struck by the powerful images of the deadly attacks of Sept. 11, 2001, when 19 al-Qaeda terrorists hijacked four American passenger planes, turning them into lethal bombs, as they targeted key sites in our country.

I was on a plane to New Orleans Baptist Theological Seminary when the tragedy struck. After landing in New Orleans, all flights were canceled. In fact, the handful of trustees who had flown in for a committee meeting could not get a bus, train, plane, or rental car out of the city. Fortunately, by Friday of that week, we were able to secure a rental car through the efforts of President Chuck Kelley.

During our time on campus, we prayed, attended chapel services, had a couple of meetings, but mostly were fixed on the television reports continually being telecast about the attacks.

It all seemed so surreal, and yet it stirred my emotions deeply.

The twin towers in New York were hit at 8:46 a.m. and 9:03 a.m. The Pentagon was struck at 9:37 a.m. — and at 10:03 a.m., the fourth hijacked plane, which many believed was headed for either the Capitol or the White House, crashed in a field in rural Pennsylvania when brave passengers rushed the hijackers. Everyone on all four planes plus over 2,000 more were killed that day.

The results of this horror were felt around the world — some rejoiced, but most rallied behind America. A headline in the French newspaper, LeMonde's, read, "We are all Americans now." President George W. Bush responded with decisive action and told the world that the U.S. would hunt down the terrorists behind the attacks. His poll numbers skyrocketed from a 55 percent favorable rating before Sept. 11 to 90 percent on Sept. 12, the highest ever recorded for a president.

U.S. military forces attacked Afghanistan where al-Qaeda had its best training bases and began the war on terrorism. Within a few months, thousands of terrorists were killed or captured and their leaders went into hiding. One report confirmed that Osama Bin Laden, the leader of al-Qaeda, had "disastrously misjudged" the will of America to fight.

On the evening of Sept. 11, 150 members of Congress gathered together on the steps of the Capitol Building. Speaker of the House Dennis Hastert said to the throng of media gathered that the Congress was united, and that "those who brought this evil deed will pay the price." As the members of Congress began to disperse, some spontaneously started to sing, "God Bless America," and immediately the rest joined that unusual choir.

In the days that followed, Billy Graham spoke at the National Cathedral to a packed house of the nation's leaders. Students and teachers prayed in our public schools all across our land without giving it a second thought. Services, gatherings, prayer meetings, etc., were held. It seemed like revival was in the air, and that this tragedy was going to be used by God for our spiritual awakening.

But it was short-lived, and our nation is in greater need of revival now than then. Our culture has shifted further away from God and His Word than we could have imagined on that fateful day in 2001.

We need a great movement of God in our nation — nothing less will suffice. It may happen, or it may not. However, the church of the Lord Jesus Christ cannot shrink from our calling to be the salt and light of this land. We may never see Congress sing "God Bless America" on the steps of the Capitol again, but we can be voices for truth and lives that truly seek first God's kingdom and His righteousness. We may feel like we cannot do much — but God can, and He has chosen to work through His faithful and believing people.

I don't think those of us who lived through the 9/11 experience will ever forget it, and I hope we will never forget to stay focused on the Sovereign Lord who can do exceedingly more than we ask or think. The kind of sincere prayers that were offered then are needed now.

October 2019

Don't Overlook Pastor Appreciation

The pastorate can often be a rewarding experience, but it can also be a discouraging valley. Far too many pastors suffer from depression, and most of them go untreated. When I first came to The Courier, I wrote a three-part series on pastoral burnout, suicide, and forced termination. South Carolina was the leader in all three categories at the time. Some progress has been made, but not enough.

Clergy Appreciation Month is October, and the second Sunday of the month is recognized as Pastor Appreciation Day. It is an opportunity for church members to encourage with gratitude the pastor and other staff members whom God has called to serve and lead the church.

The idea for a pastoral appreciation month and day came from Hallmark Greeting Cards in 1992 and Focus on the Family about the same time. Hallmark began selling cards for pastors in 2002. While a card is good, don't stop there! Be a source of encouragement to your pastor and build him up, support him, and value him. Monetary gifts are important, too. Most pastors are definitely not overpaid!

First Timothy 5:17 says, "Let the elders who rule well be

considered worthy of double honor, especially those who work hard at preaching and teaching." A pastor who leads genuinely, serves others deliberately, studies diligently, prepares ardently, prays fervently, and preaches powerfully is indeed a blessing to people in the church he serves. He often works long hours, and much of what he does goes unnoticed by church members.

What can you do for your pastor? Love and support him. Embrace his family with kindness and understanding (he often misses time with his family because he is helping someone in the congregation). As a church, give him some extra time off. Volunteer to babysit his children so he and his wife can have a night out. Aside from an official gift from the church, set up a basket or baskets and ask people to give the family a personal handwritten message with a gift card or money enclosed.

William James, sometimes referred to as the father of psychology in America, once wrote, "The deepest principle in human nature is the craving to be appreciated." Most pastors serve because they have been called by God. But pastors and staff are like everyone else: They, too, need to be appreciated. It is not enough simply to know you appreciate them — show them. Your words of encouragement can lift their spirits. Telling them that you pray for them regularly can really bless their souls.

I researched some Christian superstar preachers recently and discovered what their estimated net worth was. It was astounding. Some as high as $40 million! But, for the rest of the preachers and pastors, their financial worth is not nearly as high as their spiritual worth. They do many things for us, but most of all they accurately feed us God's truth. They probably do not push for recognition or reward, but they are deserving. The benefits of their work may be out of this world, but expressions of appreciation and gratitude should certainly be shown in this world and among those they serve.

October is the month to show pastors your appreciation in meaningful and tangible ways. But every month is the time to support, love, and value the ministers of God who lead you.

FEBRUARY 2020

God's Adventurous Missionary

Hattie Gardner was an exceptional follower of Jesus Christ.
I preached a series of "revival" services at Gum Branch Baptist Church, Hartsville, in the fall of 1981. During that week, I got to meet and spend some time with Miss Hattie. She became a missionary in 1935 and retired at the age of 70 after serving 38 years in Nigeria.

She invited the pastor at that time, Bill James, and me to lunch at her home. He tried to prepare me for what to expect, but I was touched deeply by what I saw. She lived in a tiny mobile home with just the basic necessities. I was struck that the dinnerware and glasses did not match and assumed this faithful servant of God was now living in poverty. She was kind and caring as we talked, and her love for missions was clearly at the core of her being. I left that lunch with sorrow in my heart that one of God's choice servants had to live this way. I did not know the rest of the story.

During her years in retirement, she served God as WMU director and children's Sunday school teacher at Gum Branch. She also gave generously and sacrificially to missions with the money she received from her pension and speaking engagements in churches. She said of those gifts, "You need not be praising me. I'm trying to do what every Christian should do — putting God first." At five feet tall, she was not an imposing figure, but carried an unforgettable personality coupled with a passionate commitment to Jesus Christ.

She grew up in McBee and became somewhat of a legend in Nigeria as a missionary known for her determination to do what others thought was impossible for her to do. When she was being interviewed by the Foreign Mission Board (now International Mission Board) as a potential missionary, she was told she was too small for the rigorous life in Africa. Her reply was classic: "God made me, and He knew my size when He called me to be a missionary." She received her appointment as a missionary. This type of spiritual spunk and unrelenting devotion to missions led her to a remote part of Africa — where she pulled her mobile home with a Land Rover from village to village, serving God and reaching people.

In 1982, the Sunday School Board (now Lifeway) published a book in their "Meet The Missionary Series" titled, "Hattie Gardner: Determined Adventurer." I bought a copy but must have given it to someone along my own spiritual journey.

She died Sept. 18, 1985, and left in her will money to be used for missions causes. Charitable trusts were established with the following amounts: $18,996 for foreign missions and the same amount for home missions; Gum Branch Baptist Church, Bethea Baptist Home, and Baptist Hospital of Columbia were each given $6,331.99.

At Gum Branch, the amount of the fund grew over the years, managed by the Baptist Foundation of South Carolina, to over $35,000. This past December, the church gave $20,000 from that fund to the Lottie Moon Christmas Offering during a special service honoring the legacy of Hattie Gardner. Ken Owens, SCBC missions mobilization team leader, Laurie Register, South Carolina WMU director, and Joe Willard, Welsh Neck Baptist associational mission strategist, all took part in the service.

Hattie Gardner was a spiritual giant in a small physical body. She sacrificed so she could help others reach people for Christ. What a legacy. What an example. What a challenge! Hopefully, who she was and what she did will cause us to pause and ask ourselves, "What am I doing?"

August 2020

It's Time to Rejoice!

It is time for God's people to rejoice!

In America, we have a divided nation, a raging pandemic, racial tensions, economic turbulence, and an election year creating bitterly divisive and ungodly rhetoric. However, those things are not the reason we need to rejoice.

We need to rejoice because it is God's will, and it is good for us.

Galatians 5:22 says the "fruit of the Spirit is joy." Joy is what God's Spirit can produce in us. Then, we should express the joy He puts in us — regardless of the circumstances. Philippians 4:4 says, "Rejoice in the Lord always; again I will say, rejoice!"

Rabbi Jonathan Cohn, a Messianic Jew, is calling for a Sacred Assembly for Sept. 26 at the National Mall in Washington, D.C. James Dobson, founder of Focus on the Family, is promoting it.

Cohn invites us to think about the fall of Israel and later Judah, and particularly about the prophet Habakkuk. He says, "Now is the window of time we have to repent — then judgment."

Habakkuk desperately wanted revival to come to Judah. He begged and pleaded with God to send it. He became frustrated when God did not do it. God was going to send a wicked and pagan nation to destroy Judah. Habakkuk could not understand how a nation much more wicked than Judah would be allowed to destroy His chosen people. Judah needed to repent of her wickedness, but repeated calls from the prophets produced no repentance. The story of Habakkuk is this prophet's personal struggle for revival and God's revelation of what was really going to happen. Finally, in the closing three verses of the book (3:17-19), Habakkuk changes. He begins to rejoice — not because of the calamity that was coming, but in the God who rules over it all.

He said, "Though the fig tree should not blossom, and there be no fruit on the vines, though the yield of the olive should fail and the fields produce no food, though the flock should be cut off from the fold, and there be no cattle in the stalls, yet I will exult in the Lord, I will rejoice in the God of my salvation. The Lord God is my strength, and He has made my feet like hinds' feet, and he makes me walk on my high places."

He got it! You and I need to get it, too. It's not about ignoring our present difficulties, but about focusing above everything else on the God who rules. Bad times were definitely coming, and Habakkuk could not stop it — but he could rejoice in the God who is sovereign. The circumstances did not get better for Judah, but instead got worse. The change Habakkuk wanted did not come, but the change he needed came in the nick of time. He changed.

Where do we go from here in our lives, given the current realities we face? The options are many, but the best is to bow before God in submission and listen to His Word. Like Habakkuk, things may not change. In fact, they may get worse. But we will be changed — and through expressing the Spirit-produced joy in us, others will be changed, too.

I hope a cure for COVID-19 comes soon, and I hope a successful vaccine is available in the near future. I hope races can live together in harmony and peace, and I hope our economy improves so people can enjoy the blessing of this life. I hope our politicians can learn how to behave like civil human beings and not whiny children. Most of all, I hope you and I can learn to yield to God's Spirit, who will produce His fruit in us. From the joy we receive, I hope we can rejoice (express it) in our words, songs, sermons, conversations, prayers and countenance.

Where do we go from here? Let's start at the top with God and then work our way through whatever lies before us, rejoicing in Him as we go.

DECEMBER 2020

One Solitary Life

There is a piece of prose that has grown in popularity since its inception in 1926. It is simply titled, "One Solitary Life." I first came across this in 1971 while taking a New Testament survey course at Anderson University. It is quoted by H.I. Hester in his book, "The Heart of the New Testament." He attributed it to Phillips

Brooks, but Brooks was not the author. Over the years, it has been recorded by various singers like Bill Anderson, Robert Goulet, and others. It has appeared on Christmas cards, in magazines and books, and on digital platforms. President Ronald Reagan read it to a group of children gathered at the White House in 1982. He said, "I think it describes the meaning of Christmas."

There are several versions of the composition (I stopped counting at 15), each slightly different from the other. Throughout the years, even to the present, it is often ascribed to an "unknown author." However, the author was a Baptist pastor named James Allen Francis. He became a pastor at 21 and served in ministry until his death in 1928 at age 64. After writing the first version, while serving as pastor of First Baptist Church of Los Angeles, he made some minor changes to it the following year. It is reported that the original version was part of a sermon he preached.

You may have encountered this short essay in some form or fashion. I want to include it here as a way of wishing each of you a blessed Christmas and a great New Year:

"He was born in an obscure village, the child of a peasant woman. He grew up in another village where He worked in a carpenter shop until He was thirty. Then for three years, He was an itinerant preacher.

"He never owned a home. He never wrote a book. He never went to college. He never visited a big city. He never travelled more than two hundred miles from the place where He was born. He did none of the things usually associated with greatness. He had no credentials but Himself.

"While still a young man, the tide of private opinion turned against Him. His friends ran away. One of them denied Him. He was turned over to His enemies. He went through the mockery of a trial. He was nailed to a cross between two thieves. As He was dying, His executioners gambled for the only piece of property He had — His coat.

"When He was dead, He was laid in a borrowed grave through the pity of a friend.

"Nineteen centuries have come and gone, and today He is the centerpiece of the human race and the leader of mankind's progress. All the armies that have ever marched, all the navies that have ever sailed, all the parliaments that have ever sat, all the kings that ever reigned put together have not affected the life of mankind on earth as powerfully as that one solitary life."

The Apostle Paul wrote in Philippians 2:5-11: "Have this attitude in yourselves which was also in Christ Jesus, who, although He existed in the form of God, did not regard equality with God a thing to be grasped, but emptied Himself, taking the form of a bond-servant, and being made in the likeness of men. And being found in appearance as a man, He humbled Himself by becoming obedient to the point of death, even death on a cross. Therefore also, God highly exalted Him, and bestowed on Him the name which is above every name, that at the name of Jesus every knee should bow, of those who are in heaven, and on earth, and under the earth, and that every tongue should confess that Jesus Christ is Lord, to the glory of God the Father."

Jesus came, and He is coming again. What a privilege it is to know Him through the new birth, follow Him daily, experience His unmatched forgiveness, and serve Him as King of Kings and Lord of Lords. This year, 2020, has been a tumultuous time, yet our Lord continues to show us His love, faithfulness, and truth. To Him be the glory, honor, and praise that is due Him — especially as we approach this upcoming and unusual holiday season.

March 2021

Angels and Death

Hebrews 9:27 says that "it is appointed for men to die once … ." Death is a reality we cannot escape, but it is also a transition to a greater life we cannot afford to deny.

I have had cancer surgery, followed a year later by radiation treatments and chemo infusions. I really want to see my grandchildren grow up. That may be selfish, but I will admit that I love them dearly. When I shared with my radiation oncologist that I wanted to live long enough to celebrate my 50th wedding anniversary with my patient, loving and godly wife, he said basically he thought that should happen (our 50th is in six years).

Then, I told him I wanted to see all four of my grandchildren graduate from high school. His reply was, "It's good to have goals." I took his observations to mean that six years was a very real possibility, but that 16 years was "iffy." I may not have the blessing to watch them all graduate, but I want to see all of them come to know Christ as Savior. That is something I pray for every night.

As I have pondered death off and on over the past two years, I have also grown more secure in what happens at death. I recently completed my book on angels, and it is going through the final edits now. Angels are so wonderful — one appeared in my life 24 years ago during a medical event when I was returning from an overseas mission trip. Angels, I am convinced, will be present at our time of death, and one or more will escort us into the presence of Jesus.

In the story of the rich man and Lazarus in Luke 16, the rich man died and lifted up his eyes in the torment of Hades. When Lazarus died, however, "he was carried away by angels to Abraham's bosom" (v. 22). As I researched and read trusted Christian scholars, preachers and writers, it became clear that they saw in this verse a picture of what happens when a believer dies.

Billy Graham wrote, "When my time to die comes, an angel will be there to comfort me. He will give me peace and joy even at that most critical hour, and usher me into the presence of God, and I will dwell with the Lord forever. Thank God for the ministry of His blessed angels."

The old spiritual "Swing Low, Sweet Chariot" captures the confidence of believers at death. "I looked over Jordan and what did I see, coming for to carry me home! A band of angels coming after me, coming for to carry me home."

When Charles Haddon Spurgeon, the great British preacher, was dying in 1892, he said, "I can hear them coming! Don't you hear them? This is my coronation day. I can see chariots. I'm ready to board!"

Death is real, but it is also a passageway to our heavenly home and into the presence of God forever. That we will die is a fact. How we die is the question. We can die in faith anticipating the transition to a greater life, or we can die clinging to life in this present world. No believer dies alone. That thought can be powerfully comforting to families that have relatives who died alone from COVID.

In far too many cases, caring friends and loving family members could not be with their Christian loved one when he or she passed. I am confident that Jesus was waiting, and angels were there to comfort and be with them as they exited this life and entered the next. Even if no human being is around, an angel or angels will be there when we die. They will escort us into the presence of the King of kings and Lord of lords.

There is a certain sadness when we contemplate our death. We look at the world around us and see so many things that bring us happiness and joy. I want to see my grandchildren grow up, and I want to celebrate 50 years of marriage to my loving wife. I want to see all my grandchildren born again and serving Christ before I die. I want to live as long as I can, but, above everything, I want to die resting in the peace that Jesus gives.

Hebrews 12:1 says, "[L]et us run with endurance the race that is set before us …." One day our endurance will dissipate, and our race will end. But there will be a new life waiting for us where endurance will never wane.

Death is inevitable. Heaven is real. Jesus is Savior. Angels are an integral part of God's plan. Hebrews 9:27 says the angels are "ministering spirits sent out to render service for the sake of those who will inherit salvation." They serve us in this life and are with us in our journey through death. We can live with confidence until we die and when we die.

June 2021

We Need Godly Fathers

The absence of fathers in homes has a powerful and damaging impact, while the active involvement of fathers with their children is positively related to good outcomes for kids that helps them throughout life. We need fathers who are physically present in the home, emotionally involved with their children, and spiritually strong in the Christian faith. We need godly fathers in this country now more than ever.

Through the efforts of organized liberal forces, parents face a tremendous challenge in raising their children in this powerful and growing atmosphere of wickedness. The invasion into our homes by misinformed government powers or the immoral values of culture warriors puts us in a position where we cannot afford to ignore what is happening. Our homes are under attack. In fact, the fundamental idea of a man and a woman marrying and having children is scorned by far too many in this culture. Many evil and insidious dangers face our kids and grandkids. They deserve parents, especially dads, who will stand in the truth and model before their kids character, truth and devotion. They need protectors, not compromisers!

We cannot be with our children 24 hours a day, but we can pray for them around the clock and we can be involved in their lives virtually every day. James 5:16 reminds us that "the effective prayer of a righteous man can accomplish much." It has been my practice to pray for my children every day, then my sons-in-law, and I have now added my four grandchildren to my petitions before God's throne. Dads and granddads can have a huge impact in the lives of their kids and grandkids through prayer, which is an immeasurable asset in their development.

Father's Day can be a time to pause and realize the importance of fathers. It can be a time to give thanks to God for good dads and a special opportunity to honor them with our lives — both those fathers those who are still with us, and those who are deceased.

While the observance of Father's Day is a holiday recognized in the United States every third Sunday in June, it is not a federal holiday. But it is a time to celebrate the men who fathered us, especially those who sacrificed for us and took the time to teach, lead and correct us. I realize some children do not have dads, and others have dads who are abusive or absent. These children need our prayers and attention, and, as God leads us, our intervention. One dad said he could not be a father to children outside his family, but he could be an involved father figure in their lives.

For a child, love is spelled T-I-M-E. One dad made a lasting difference in his son's life by promising his child one hour a day to do whatever he wanted with his dad. Looking back on the time spent he with his dad, the grown son said, "It is the greatest gift I ever had in my life."

This Father's Day, remember your dad. If he is alive, spend time with him either through a phone call, social media, or, best of all, in person. There are plenty of dads who abandon their posts while chasing their dream, a hobby, or money. But if your dad, imperfect as we all are, has demonstrated to you over the years his love for you, remember him with respect and honor his name.

It has been observed that being a father is too often a title without a commitment to fathering. When this happens, men devalue their children and imprint them with various feelings of unworthiness, guilt, pain and anger. Those scars can last a lifetime.

Our families in America are hurting, and the very structure of the family is being attacked and severely damaged. We need godly fathers who stay the course and provide examples of love, integrity, and commitment to their children.

If you have a good father, touch his life in a special way on Father's Day. Your time is likely more valuable to him than any material gift.

If you feel the need to show your love with some type of tangible gift, avoid obsessing about the monetary value of a material present. As one small boy said, "Father's Day is like Mother's Day, only you don't spend as much."

To all of you dads and granddads who are still involved in the lives of your kids and grandkids, have a happy and blessed Father's Day. May your tribe increase!

July 2021

The Greatest Generation

With this July issue we are paying tribute to members of the "Greatest Generation." Particularly, we are focusing on those who served in the military, especially those who fought in the Pacific and European theaters of war. The Fourth of July is a national holiday, and we can certainly pause and give thanks to God for those who gave their lives for the freedoms we enjoy.

Over 16 million Americans served in World War II. According to the Department of Veterans Affairs, there were only 325,574 remaining in 2020. That number is less than 300,000 today. On average, 296 veterans die each day. The average age for a soldier in 1944 was 26, but many young men enlisted when they were 17. In 2020, there were 4,000 World War II veterans living in South Carolina. In the next few years, the Greatest Generation will be gone.

Those of this generation who are living today have seen more change than any group of people in United States history. They produced a birth rate so large that their children became known as the Baby Boomers, born between 1946 and 1964 — over 76 million of us.

In what was called the war to end all wars, they left their homes in defense of freedom. True stories from that group abound. Twenty-year-old Guy Whidden was a paratrooper and machine gunner with the 502nd, 101st Airborne Division, who jumped at 300 feet in the attack at Omaha Beach. A bullet hit the prayer book in his pocket on his way down and stopped at the last page. The night before the jump, he cut his hair into a mohawk to intimidate the Germans. He was ordered to cut it before the mission began. In 2020, at age 96, he had his hair cut into a mohawk again as a tribute to his fallen comrades.

In that same attack, the 320th Barrage Balloon Battalion, an African-American unit (the military was segregated at this time), fought bravely against the German forces. Medic Waverly Woodson Jr. was wounded but continued helping over 200 soldiers for 30 nonstop hours before he collapsed from exhaustion.

Charles Norman Shay was a Penobscot Indian and medic assigned to the First Division 16th Infantry Regiment. He said his "duty was to save lives." Bullets were hitting all around him on Omaha Beach during the D-Day invasion, but he was not injured. However, 65 percent of the men in his unit were killed.

Over a million American soldiers were killed in that global war. They fought for others. Over 6 million Jews were exterminated by the Nazis. Many more would have perished if the U.S. and other nations had not stopped the evil madness of Hitler-led Germany.

When I think of the sacrifices that millions of people have made to give us the greatest opportunity to live free and blessed lives, I am humbled. When I realize God is a sovereign God and chose to bless America, I am amazed. Underneath the patriotism surrounding Fourth of July celebrations is the realization that we are blessed in order to be a blessing. Our nation today, like our Southern Baptist Convention, is divided. We face a culture that is driving us to, basically, commit suicide as a nation.

I am old enough to believe that this nation came into existence by the grace of God and that if we continue for years into the future, it will be because of the forgiveness of God for our disregard of His truth and His blessings. The true church needs to repent for our sins, return to a healthy relationship with Christ, and reengage a culture that seeks to eliminate our views and beliefs from the mainstream of education, government, and even the family. Now is not the time to retreat into silence or despair, but to take a stand in the truth with the disposition of love.

I like songs such as "God Bless America," "America the Beautiful," and "The Star-Spangled Banner." But I love songs that tell the story of Jesus and His amazing love. The sacrifice of Jesus on the cross is greater than the great sacrifices of the Greatest Generation. I think most of them would agree.

Celebrate the Fourth of July holiday and remember those who fought and died to give us this liberty, but, above all, stop and thank God for His Son and the eternal freedom He gives us through the new birth.

AUGUST 2021

THE THINKING CHRISTIAN

Pastor and theologian Alistair Begg said, "We need to do what the Bible has always entrusted us to do: Think."

In different ways and in varying degrees, we are all thinkers. It is a God-given ability, and the Christian faith is a thinking faith. Martyn Lloyd-Jones wrote, "The whole trouble with a man of little faith is that he does not think." However, we are almost always thinking — even when we are asleep. The problem is not that we do not think, but how we think and what we think about.

Thoughts are the products of the mind, and they always have consequences. Proverbs 23:7a says, "As he thinks (or reasons) within himself, so he is." Our mind is the faculty by which we think, feel, and act. Feelings and behaviors follow thoughts. Jonathan Edwards defined the will of a person, not as an entity of itself, but as the mind choosing. He stated that our choices are determined not by our wills directly, but by our minds choosing to will a choice. It is our minds, not our feelings, that direct our lives.

Christian psychologist Archibald Hart wrote in his book, "Habits of the Mind," that thoughts are the "essential ingredients for living and underlie all our actions and feelings. Research has shown that one's thought life influences every aspect of one's being." He emphasizes that our emotions can never transcend our thoughts.

Augustine observed, "Everything that is believed is believed after being preceded by thoughts." He believed that our lives consist not of contemplation or action, but both.

The Christian faith is a thinking faith, and, as followers of Jesus, our lives should be characterized by at least four basic and growing dynamics:

1. Turn away from evil. First Thessalonians 5:22 says, "Abstain from every form of evil."
2. Be accurate with Scripture. Second Timothy 2:15 states, "Be diligent to present yourself approved to God as a workman who does not need to be ashamed, accurately handling the word of truth."
3. Live in the truth. In John 14:6, Jesus said, "I am the way, and the truth, and the life." In His high priestly prayer, just before He went through the agony of Gethsemane and the brutality of the cross, He prayed in John 17:17, "Sanctify them in the truth; thy word is truth."
4. Experience continuing transformation. Romans 12:2 counsels us, "Do not be conformed to this world, but be transformed by the renewing of your mind, so that you may prove what the will of God is, that which is good and acceptable and perfect."

Hart writes, "Who you are as a Christian can be no better and no worse than the thoughts you entertain in your head." Philippians 4:8 says, "Whatever is true, whatever is honorable, whatever is right, whatever is pure, whatever is lovely, whatever is of good repute, if there is any excellence and if anything worthy of praise, dwell on these things."

The French philosopher René Descartes famously said, "I think, therefore I am." He explained that sentence by noting that we cannot doubt our existence because we exist. With apologies to Descartes, believers could say, "I am a Christian, therefore I think rightly (biblically)."

The mind can produce all sorts of thoughts, imaginations, ideas, and impressions. But the mind that thinks God's truth and continually applies that truth in life is a blessed person like the person described in Psalm 1:2 who "delights in the Law of the Lord, and in His Law he meditates day and night."

Memorizing Scripture is important. Understanding what we memorize is even more important. Both memorization and understanding are products of the mind. When we meditate on the Word, we have an inner conversation with ourselves, and we focus, ponder, and think on the verse or verses of Scripture before us.

The Christian faith is a thinking faith, but it is more than just a thinking faith — it is a growing relationship with God through Christ. As followers of Jesus, *that* we think is not the objective but *how* we think. First Corinthians 14:20 says, "Brethren, do not be children in your thinking; yet in evil be infants, but in your thinking be mature."

God has planned good works for us to do (Ephesians 2:10), but to recognize them and do them in a manner that glorifies God, we need God Himself empowering us. Ephesians 3:20 describes God as "Him who is able to do far more abundantly beyond all that we ask or think, according to the power that works within us." In order to accept that verse, we must believe it is true. That involves thinking. The Christian faith is, indeed, a thinking faith.

SEPTEMBER 2021

To Boomer

Our departed little boy, Boomer

Last month our Shih Tzu dog, Boomer, passed away. My wife and I cried and grieved painfully as we watched him die. As we reminisced about his 12-year journey with us, our tears flowed even more.

Boomer was special in many ways. We looked exhaustively for a puppy before we found Boomer. When we finally saw him, my wife, Anne, said, "I think we have found our dog."

That began a journey filled with good memories. He delighted to lay on his back in my lap as I sat on the sofa and watched television. He and our other Shih Tzu, Sassy, always greeted me when I came home, regardless of the time.

We projected onto Boomer (aka, Boom Boom or Boomie) our human qualities. We had conversations with Boomer, and it was always amusing. I was a guest on Tony Beam's radio program when he asked me what my next book project was. I told him on air that I was thinking about a title, "Conversations with Boomer." When he asked what it was about, I told him it was about our "conversations" with our dog. I then had to explain what I meant. He quickly pivoted and moved on in our interview.

Boomer suffered during the last three weeks of his life. He had severe arthritis and a major flare up that left him without the ability to walk or even stand. I carried him in my arms whenever he needed something. He was examined by two different veterinarians, and both recommended "putting him down." Not wanting him to suffer any longer, we took the vets' advice. We stroked his head, looked into his eyes, and comforted him as he breathed his last breath. Our sweet boy was gone, and we cried and cried.

I thought about writing a tribute to him that would be titled, "Boomer: The Dog, the Myth, The Legend." In short, we loved Boomer. Sassy is smaller than he was and has an attitude that matches her name. She will turn 12 in November.

I wanted to get another puppy after Boomer died, but Anne said no. I continued to look at the possibilities, knowing that she had to want another dog herself. On my birthday, she gave me a card with some money and a handwritten message inside: "You can put this toward a puppy."

I immediately jumped into action — and within two days, we adopted a three-month-old Shihpoo, who we named Buddy. He is a "designer dog," bred from a Shih Tzu and a Toy Poodle. He is a true bundle of energy — smart, playful, somewhat mischievous, and so good-looking. We are in the process of training him (or learning how he wants to train us). Sassy keeps him in line, and Buddy is quickly learning that she is the alpha dog at our house. I will admit that I am a dog man — and at my age now, I am a small dog man.

I would not dare say that dogs go to heaven, but I do recall a movie called, "All Dogs Go to Heaven." Of course, it was not based on Scripture. For us, our dogs are a challenge, a blessing, and sometimes an annoyance — like some people.

Why would I take up this space to write about Boomer and our dogs? With all the sin, evil and destruction going on in the world today, I thought it might offer a distraction, some humor, or even encouragement for some of you.

Second Samuel 12 records the prophet Nathan telling King David a parable. Without going into the most important message in the parable, I wanted to share with you the description of a pet lover. Verse 3 says, "The poor man had nothing except one little ewe lamb which he bought and nourished; and it grew up together with him and his children. It would eat of his bread and drink of his cup and lie in his bosom and was like a daughter to him." In Nathan's parable, there was also a rich man who had a "great many flocks and herds," but he took the poor man's pet and butchered it for a meal. When King David heard, he was furious. Most of us are, too, when we read the story.

Pets provide us with benefits we simply cannot calculate. We get so attached to them that when death takes them from us, we grieve.

Here's to Boomer, gone but never forgotten — and to Buddy, who won't let us forget him! And to Sassy, who helps us maintain discipline in our pack.

May blessings large and small come your way with or without a pet.

December 2021

The Buckley Legacy

Seth Buckley has been a minister of students for most of the years he has been in ministry. He is, however, much more than a title. He has a powerful and beautiful voice, which is on full display when he sings the great songs of the faith with passion and emphasis. His combination of unique abilities is, in part, a tribute to his late father, Sid Buckley.

The elder Buckley became known as the "baritone of the South" and carried his tremendous talent to 43 states, singing in churches and conventions. His family was often with him on his journeys. He served on university faculties and worked as a music minister in local churches.

I had a conversation with Sid Buckley Jr. following Seth's farewell service at Spartanburg First Baptist Church. His dad started out life in a sharecropper's shack in Mississippi. Sid Jr. said his dad applied for the Doctor of Philosophy degree in vocal performance at Florida State University, following his graduation from New Orleans Baptist Theological Seminary. He was told he would need to pass a proficiency test in three foreign languages to qualify for the program. He spent three months locked away in his study, learning three languages on his own. He passed the test, and, as they say, the rest is history.

Seth said his dad sang the national anthem for Florida State University home games — without a microphone! That reminds me of the time Sid was sitting in the rear balcony at a pastors' or evangelism conference at First Baptist, Columbia. The worship leader was directing the congregation of mostly pastors in a hymn when he spotted Sid in the balcony. He stopped the music and said, "Dr. Buckley, would you sing that next verse?" Without hesitation, a hymn book, or a microphone, Sid stood up and filled the auditorium with a worshipful and melodious sound. Everyone was moved, and, at the same time, impressed by the ability of this man of God.

Sid Jr. said his dad used to tell his family, "Put the plow on, and God will use you." He was an outdoorsman and enjoyed hunting, fishing, and plowing. Seth added, "He devoted his gifts and talents to lift up the name of Jesus, and he loved to see his children and grandchildren serving Jesus."

Sid had a serious back injury and lived with chronic pain most of his life, the last 20 years being especially difficult. But singing helped him. When the family would gather at his house, he would say, "Let's sing some of the old hymns." Since all the family was musically talented in multiple ways, they always joined in. When they would sing, neighbors would often sit on their porches to enjoy the concert.

Sid died in December 2017 at the age of 81. Seth spoke and sang "How Great Thou Art" at his dad's funeral.

In some important ways, Sid was an underdog. It is more than interesting that his son, Seth, is a champion for the underdog. Rather than give up on troubled youth, he goes the second mile with them and has now made the transition to work with them at Fire Pit Ranch with his son, Jacob. Seth is convinced that the most conflicted, disadvantaged, or oppressed young person can rise to greatness through the power of God's grace.

To top it off, he can sing. As my wife and I listened to him sing "The Anchor Holds" at First Baptist, Spartanburg, recently, she turned to me and said, "That man can really — I mean really — sing!" Following the service that day, I said to him, "You are Sid Buckley's son." He has a wonderful voice, and it is just one of the gifts in his talent package that he utilizes in serving the God he loves. During a solo, when I see him clench his fist, raise his hand, or plant his foot, I know he is not just feeling the emotion of the song — he is believing it.

Seth Buckley, like his dad, is an extraordinarily gifted person. Now he begins a new chapter in his life, working with his son, Jacob, and others to mentor and disciple disadvantaged boys — most of whom are without a father figure in their lives. We will watch with great interest as he tightens the plow and follows the path in which God leads him.

Sid prayed on his wedding day that the children God may give them would bring God glory.

That prayer has been, and is still being, answered today — not only in his children, but also in his grandchildren.

January 2022

Resolutions or Renewals?

Instead of making New Year's resolutions this year (that we typically do not keep), let me challenge you to make a renewed commitment to simply obey the counsel found in the Bible.

We can plan, prepare, and reminisce, but the greatest challenge is for each of us to live one day at a time. We all can read, study, and meditate on the Word (Psalm 1), but we must move to the next obvious step of obeying and applying God's truth to our lives.

Instead of our natural tendency to be anxious or worried, Jesus gave us the greatest alternative to worry in Matthew 6:33: "But seek first His kingdom and His righteousness, and all these things will be added to you." First Peter 5:7 says, "Casting all your anxiety on Him, because He cares for you."

In the last several years, I have read a different daily devotional book each year. This past year I read "My Utmost For His Highest" by Oswald Chambers. Even though I did not agree with his apparent emphasis on a second work of grace and complete sanctification resulting from the second work of grace, I did find many statements that were encouraging and helpful. If you are wondering what I am talking about, let me explain. Baptists have consistently believed that sanctification begins at the time of our new birth, continues throughout our lives, and is completed when we enter the presence of God at the conclusion of this life. We do not believe a person attains sinless perfection in this life.

There are many good devotional books that are worth reading — even if you find some statements that may be in contradiction to your beliefs. The point is to find a devotional work and commit yourself to read a daily devotional — daily. Even if you find something you do not agree with, use it as an impetus to study what you do believe by reading the Word more diligently. Read or listen to the expositions of Scripture by solid and faithful scholars, pastors, and teachers. The result will be the strengthening of your own faith.

May you enjoy a blessed 2022 and find in this new year, new opportunities to grow in Christ Jesus and serve in His name.

Here are a few important verses that I believe can help us all live for God's glory and our highest good:

- Philippians 4:4: "Rejoice in the Lord always."
- 2 Corinthians 13:11: "… rejoice, be made complete, be comforted, be like-minded, live in peace; and the God of love and peace will be with you."
- Colossians 3:2: "Set your mind on the things above, not on the things that are on earth."
- 1 Thessalonians 5:17-18: "Pray without ceasing; in everything give thanks; for this is God's will for you in Christ Jesus."
- Ephesians 6:10: "… be strong in the Lord and in the strength of His might."
- Galatians 5:16: "… walk by the Spirit, and you will not carry out the desire of the flesh."
- 1 Corinthians 15:58: "… be steadfast, immovable, always abounding in the work of the Lord, knowing that your toil is not in vain in the Lord."
- Romans 12:2: "… do not be conformed to this world, but be transformed by the renewing of your mind."
- 1 John 4:7: "… love one another, for love is from God."
- Jude 3: "… contend earnestly for the faith which was once for all delivered to the saints."
- 1 Peter 5:6-7: "… humble yourselves, therefore, under the mighty hand of God, that He may exalt you at the proper time."
- Matthew 5:16: "Let your light shine before men in such a way that they may see your good works, and glorify your Father who is in heaven."

February 2022

The Virtue of Waiting

Isaiah 40:31 says, "Yet those who wait for the Lord will gain new strength; They will mount up with wings like eagles, They will run and not get tired, They will walk and not become weary." Who you wait for is of critical importance, and learning to wait is a necessary second step in that process of obedience.

Waiting is an interesting word. It basically means to delay action or remain stationary but in readiness and expectation. It is an experience or state of watchfulness and anticipation. The challenge for all of us who follow Jesus is learning to wait patiently before Him. Unfortunately, few of us do.

There are times in life when there is nothing else we can do but wait. I do not like waiting in a line, especially when it comes to eating. Nevertheless, I occasionally have to do it — but, characteristically, I do it impatiently!

I heard about a little boy who was having trouble sitting quietly at his desk at school. Exasperated, the teacher finally said, "Stay in that seat and do not move!" He submitted but got the last word by responding, "I may be sitting on the outside, but I am standing on the inside." Our waiting or being still before God is not an occasion for rebellion in our heart. It is the opportunity to wait peacefully and patiently in our heart and in our activity.

Isaiah 64:4 tells us that God "acts in behalf of the one who waits for Him." Even when it comes to serving God, we may exhibit more impatience than patience. We suffer from what Christian psychologist Archibald Hart called "hurry disease." Instead of being calm, patient, and relaxed, we can become tense, overactive, and busy to the point of missing the lesson or blessing that can come to us from our Lord.

Psalm 130:5 says, "I wait for the Lord, my soul does wait; and in His Word do I hope." Paul wrote in Romans 8:24-25, "For in hope we have been saved, but hope that is seen is not hope; for why does one also hope for what he sees? But if we hope for what we do not see, with perseverance we wait eagerly for it." We are saved, we are being saved, and some glorious day we will experience the fulness of salvation in a new body and in the presence of God.

Waiting is God's will for us. In our daily routines, we wait for many things — but in our Christian walk, we are called to wait in expectation and faith in God. He is God; we are not. He knows more than we ever will and does more than we could ever imagine. He is in control, not us.

In his poem, "The Birds of Killingworth," Henry Wadsworth Longfellow depicts a time when the farmers decided to kill all the birds. Longfellow defended the goodness and benefits of allowing the birds to live. But the birds were slaughtered, and many of the farmers regretted it too late. Longfellow's words remind us that often the greatest thing we can do is wait: "For after all, the best thing one can do when it is raining is to let it rain." Fortunately for the villagers in Longfellow's poem, someone brought more birds of song to the village.

In an anxious world where most of us are conditioned for instant gratification, the challenge for Christians is to learn a different and better way of living. Waiting may not solve all our problems, but it will eliminate many of them. There are certainly times that call for immediate action. When that moment comes, we must respond with action. But what we learn in the times of waiting (that attitude of watchfulness and expectation) will likely condition us to be even more effective during the rarer times of crisis.

We must wait in line for a multitude of things. We have "waiting rooms" for everything, from medical needs to mechanical issues. Waiting is sewn into the fabric of life. It is not *that* we wait, but *how* we wait that is the key. Patience or endurance is learned through waiting.

Farmers prepare the soil, plant the seed, water, and nurture the soil. Then wait. It is a law engrained in nature by God Himself. Following the great flood, the Lord said, "While the earth remains, seedtime and harvest, and cold and heat, and summer and winter, and day and night shall not cease."

Times of testing are realities we all will experience. James says the testing of our faith produces endurance, patience, or steadfastness. It also involves waiting. I recall Phillips Brooks sharing a story about a parishioner who came to visit him. Brooks could not be seated but kept getting up and walking. His church member said, "Pastor, what is wrong with you?" Brooks replied, "I will tell you what's wrong with me. I am in a hurry, and God is not!"

Waiting is vitally important. We all need to become better at it so we can be more effective in our service and witness to God. Psalm 27:14 says, "Wait for the Lord; Be strong, and let your heart take courage; Yes, wait for the Lord." More times than we might imagine, waiting for the Lord may be our greatest experience of kingdom work.

March 2022

Tribute to Bill Adams

Bill Adams passed away earlier this year at age 84. He was a great friend and supporter of The Courier and a compassionate servant of Christ. He was the pastor of five different churches before serving as minister of visitation at Spartanburg First Baptist Church.

Bill and his late wife, Shirley, had two sons, two daughters, five grandchildren, and two great-grandsons. After becoming editor of The Courier, I talked with Bill many times. Sometimes he would call me and say, "I just want to encourage you."

His oldest son, Dan, served on our board of trustees for five years. Immediately following Dan's selection to our board, Bill told me, "I am so glad Dan is serving on the board of The Courier. I always wanted to serve but never got the opportunity. He will be a blessing to you." Dan was a blessing to us as a trustee. He made the initial financial contribution to our "Bill and Shirley Adams Student Internship Program" and intends to make more. When I talked with Bill about naming the internship program after him, he insisted that we name it the "Bill and Shirley Adams" fund. Why? He shared with me that the best thing that ever happened to him, apart from being saved, was his wife.

Bill was present for our "Friends of The Courier" banquets, trustee luncheons, and even sat in on a couple of our trustee meetings. Dan said, "He worked tirelessly and faithfully to share the love of Jesus with different people and different communities across the Carolinas. He gave his whole life for others to know Jesus."

He was a true friend of The Courier, and we genuinely appreciate all the work he did in helping to fund the internship program and other ministries of The Courier. He admired his wife's writing ability and was especially fond of a poem she wrote, "Behold." It was printed on the program for his funeral. I wanted to share it with you below.

Bill's love for Shirley was obvious. Today, they are together in heaven. As Dan said before the funeral for his dad, "I already miss him." We at The Courier will also miss him.

We are thankful for special friends like Bill Adams. His witness will live on through the student internship fund. If you would like to honor Bill's life by making a financial gift to the "Bill and Shirley Adams Student Internship Program," please send your check marked "Adams Internship" to The Courier, 100 Manly St., Greenville, S.C., 29601. If you prefer using a credit card, please call The Courier at (864) 232-8736 and ask for our business manager, Chris Holliday. He will be delighted to help you.

BEHOLD

Behold, if you have never forgiven, you have never loved.

If you have never felt the need to be forgiven; you have never experienced or received love, and this is lostness and/or self-righteousness. This is pride.

Therefore, may your heart, as does mine, rejoice in the Lord Jesus Christ, who at the cross paid our debt for sin.

Each day in advance, choose to forgive — even before anything happens, choose to forgive. This creates a capacity to love another.

Recognize in advance that you yourself will need to be forgiven, thereby opening a door for others to love you, respect, and honor you.

Love is giving — Jesus did this at the cross. Forgiveness is understanding that Jesus did this, too, because He understood our lostness.

Go and so live your life. Earn the right to love yourself. Be a beautiful, repeatable miracle of God.

Having crossed the bridge of life sixty-six years, tested as by fire, forgiveness works — it is love.

August 2022

The Month of August

Someone recently said, "August is sort of a nothing month." I disagree with that assumption. It is a hot month, often the hottest of the year for the people of South Carolina. Kids are going back to school and college football is ramping up for another season. The anticipation of autumn begins to influence our thoughts.

August is named after Augustus Caesar and has two birthstones: peridot and sardonyx. The flower for this month is the gladiolus from the Latin word *gladius,* which means "sword."

Aug. 12 is Vinyl Record Day and Aug. 13 is International Left-Handers Day.

August contains the dog days of summer, where there is a peak in both temperature and humidity.

Martin Luther King Jr. made his famous "I Have A Dream" speech on Aug. 28.

Our oldest and youngest daughters and our oldest grandchild were born in August.

Elvis Presley died in August 1977, three days before Anne

and I were married. August is a meaningful month for our family. Following the wedding, we traveled to St. Augustine, Fla., where we quickly discovered we had food poisoning along with several members of the wedding party. Our first three days as husband and wife were spent in separate beds feeling pretty miserable. We did eventually revive and enjoyed the rest of our honeymoon.

We enjoyed St. Augustine Beach and Jacksonville Beach — and we even visited the Fountain of Youth, where I bought an empty bottle and filled it with water from the famous fountain.

I kept it in our fridge for many years, taking a sip now and then. Anne was somewhat disgusted with my practice. Eventually, we tossed the bottle and remaining water. It did not help me stay young, but I did start losing my hair!

This year we will celebrate our 45th wedding anniversary. I shared with my radiation oncologist that I wanted to live long enough to celebrate our 50th anniversary. He encouraged me, saying, "That's very doable." Then I pushed him a little further, saying I wanted to see all my grandchildren graduate from high school. He said it was good to have goals!

I was the pastor of my first church when we got married. Anne was teaching high school algebra. In January 1977 we spent a week attending the "January Bible Study" on Romans. That was the first time I told her indirectly that I loved her. When I dropped her off at her house, I asked her to look up a Bible verse and that would explain my feelings. The next night, on our way to Bible study, she didn't say anything. I finally said, "Well, did you read the verse?" She grinned and said, "Yes, I love you, too."

By the way, the verse was 2 Corinthians 11:11: "Why? Because I do not love you? God knows I do!" This verse had nothing to do with my admission of my love for Anne, but it got the point across. Years later, she teased me about being a coward because I did not just come out and plainly say, "I love you."

We owned almost nothing as newlyweds, but we were able to get a loan and move into our first house in August.

When I proposed, we went to my study and knelt before the couch to pray. While she was praying, I very quietly slipped the diamond ring and one rose from underneath the couch. I prayed briefly, and then she opened her eyes. That's when I popped the question: "Will you marry me?" She responded with a yes and a hug.

I wasn't trying to be cheap by giving her just one rose, but with my finances following the purchase of the ring, it was about all I could afford. I did not realize it then, but over the years one rose on our anniversary became the standard — and it was a lot cheaper than a dozen!

I like August, not because it is a spectacular month, but because of all the significant things that have occurred in our lives. I was born July 31 — almost an August baby.

Here's to August — a great month!

October 2022

Gen Z Christians Show Potential

My generation, the baby boomers, has been replaced as the largest generation in American history by Generation Z, commonly referred to as Gen Z. Boomers were born between 1946 and 1964 (I am in the middle at 1953), while Gen Z individuals were born between 1997 and 2012, according to Pew Research. There are approximately 72 million of them today.

Gen Z is driven by a desire to be unique and challenge the status quo. They are digital natives, having the skill and expertise that far surpasses previous generations. In fact, some have noted that whatever you think you know about the internet, they know more! The average age a Gen Z person got their first smartphone was around 12, while their first tablet was between 10-11. They typically shun Facebook, investing their time and energy in TikTok and Instagram instead.

Despite their superior digital skills, most of them grew up in homes where their parents provided little to no direction. Their personal identity is more important to them than any group affiliation or social bond, but they often feel lonely and alone. It is estimated that over 90 percent of them are online every day. Barna Research has pointed out that 63 percent of teens agree that their devices keep them from having real conversations.

They grew up, and are growing up, in a world after the Sept. 11 attacks on our nation. Their world has never been regarded as a safe place. In their world, terrorist attacks are normal, and they tend to be less trusting of people and more trusting of technology. This generation is ready to live and work just about anywhere in the world — even though they are afraid of the dangers, conflicts, and extremism they may face.

They are racially diverse and liberal on most of the social issues of our day. They support, for example, gay and transgender rights and embrace diversity and social equality.

Gen Z is the most skeptical of any generation about various

products that are presented to them for sale. While they are less likely to own a vehicle, they are most likely to attend college. In fact, Gen Z may become the most well-educated generation yet.

What about their relationship with Jesus? Seventy-eight percent of this generation say they believe in God, or a god. One person observed, "When a Gen Z person goes all in for Jesus, the level of wholeheartedness surpasses anything I've seen yet."

Every generation is different, but Gen Z may be the most radically different generation we have ever encountered to date. Their remarkable skills and intellectual abilities, once redeemed by Christ Jesus, can become something amazing when weighed on the scales of eternity. Those who are committed to Christ can make an eternal impact on this world.

The American Bible Society stated earlier in 2022 that a large percentage of Gen Z Christians do not attend church at least once a month. But, in its latest report, the ABS observed that Gen Z led all age groups in openness to sharing their faith. They estimated that 58 percent of those in the survey were "most likely to have had spiritual conversations with three or more non-church connections in the past year." Forty-four percent of Gen Z Christians said reading the Bible "brought them closer to God."

Gen Z is the largest generation. There is significant potential in Gen Z Christians. We need to understand this generation and be God's tools in reaching them, discipling them, and encouraging them. Their great digital aptitudes may be the means through which the next great revival comes.

JUNE 2022

Keep On Keeping On

Sisters Helen Hanks, Joyce Hayes McCullough, and Juanita Loftis with Rudy Gray.

Thomas Haggai told me once, "Every morning since I was a teenager, I start the day by simply saying, 'Lord, don't let me die until I am dead!'" He was an enormously successful businessman and motivational speaker. He passed away on March 27, 2020, at the age of 89.

Some things are impressive because of longevity, strength, or size. But the most outstanding and memorable things are people who not only live long but live well. They trust Jesus, attend church, and live for His glory.

For about the last six months, I have been serving Rocky River

Baptist Church near Iva as supply pastor. The church is small but strong. It has the potential for growth and contains some remarkable people. On Mother's Day, I had my photo taken with three sisters who are some of the most faithful Christian Baptists I have met. They sit together every Sunday morning on the same pew.

On my first Sunday there, they initiated a conversation with me. They were friends with my late mother and told me how much they loved her. Every Sunday, I walk by their pew and speak with them. They always greet me with a sweet smile and a warm handshake. They are special in the best sense of that word.

I grew up in Iva and know something about nearly all the churches in the area. The church's property is in Anderson County and Abbeville County. Lake Secession is very close by. I grew up fishing, skiing, swimming, and camping around the lake. It has been a delight to serve the church during the last few months.

While we were having our photo taken, one of the sisters said, "Rudy, we consider you one of us." These sisters make you feel accepted and welcomed: Helen Hanks (95), Joyce McCullough (88), and Juanita Loftis (92). In some ways, they remind me of the giant redwoods of California. These trees can live over 1,000 years and can grow taller than the length of a football field. Year in and year out, they just keep going. They are resistant to decay and fire (a good thing for living in California). In a similar manner, these Christian ladies have lived through so much in their lifetimes and just keep on keeping on. That, in itself, is a great testimony.

I plan to retire for the second time at the end of this year after over 47 years in ministry. I don't plan to retire from serving God! In fact, I am praying now about the next opportunity He will give me. I feel like the boxer who was knocked down in the last round. He got up, shook himself off, and said, "There's still a lot of fight left in me." That is the way I feel about serving the Lord Jesus Christ.

I started out as a journalist, a sportswriter and layout man for the Anderson Independent newspaper. My time as editor of the Anderson University school paper helped prepare me for that job. From journalist to youth minister, pastor, pastor and counselor, and journalist again, I have been blessed by the sovereign hand of our great God. I have some regrets, hurts, sorrows, and failures, but I have never been forsaken by Christ Jesus. I believe the Bible and can bear witness to the truth of Romans 10:11 in my journey: "Whoever believes in Him will not be disappointed."

The faithful sisters at Rocky River Baptist have been a blessing to see each Sunday. I think they illustrate to us the call to be faithful. Luke 9:62 says, "Jesus said to them, 'No one, after putting his hand to the plow and looking back, is fit for the kingdom of God.'" From one plowman to another, let's keep on plowing until we meet our Lord at death or in the air when He raptures His church. Either way: Keep on keeping on! God is faithful, and it is the calling of each one of His children to be faithful to Him.

www.ingramcontent.com/pod-product-compliance
Lightning Source LLC
Chambersburg PA
CBHW061443040426
42450CB00007B/1192